LAYMAN'S LIBRARY OF CHRISTIAN DOCTRINE

God's Work of Salvation

BERT DOMINY

BROADMAN PRESS
Nashville, Tennessee

© Copyright 1986 • Broadman Press

All rights reserved

4216-38

ISBN: 0-8054-1638-2

Dewey Decimal Classification: 234

Subject Heading: SALVATION

Library of Congress Catalog Card Number: 83-71264

Printed in the United States of America

Library of Congress Cataloging-in-Publication Data

Dominy, Bert, 1938-
  God's work of salvation.

  Includes index.
  1. Salvation.   I. Title.
BT751.2.D65   1986   234   83-71264
ISBN 0-8054-1638-2

TO
Jo, Steven, and Susan

Foreword

The *Layman's Library of Christian Doctrine* in sixteen volumes covers the major doctrines of the Christian faith.

To meet the needs of the lay reader, the *Library* is written in a popular style. Headings are used in each volume to help the reader understand which part of the doctrine is being dealt with. Technical terms, if necessary to the discussion, will be clearly defined.

The need for this series is evident. Christians need to have a theology of their own, not one handed to them by someone else. The *Library* is written to help readers evaluate and form their own beliefs based on the Bible and on clear and persuasive statements of historic Christian positions. The aim of the series is to help laymen hammer out their own personal theology.

The books range in size from 140 pages to 168 pages. Each volume deals with a major part of Christian doctrine. Although some overlap is unavoidable, each volume will stand on its own. A set of the sixteen-volume series will give a person a complete look at the major doctrines of the Christian church.

Each volume is personalized by its author. The author will show the vitality of Christian doctrines and their meaning for everyday life. Strong and fresh illustrations will hold the interest of the reader. At times the personal faith of the authors will be seen in illustrations from their own Christian pilgrimage.

Not all laymen are aware they are theologians. Many may believe they know nothing of theology. However, every person believes something. This series helps the layman to understand what he believes and to be able to be "prepared to make a defense to anyone who calls him to account for the hope that is in him" (1 Pet. 3:15, RSV).

Contents

1

The Human Problem

A drama is easier to understand if you don't miss the prologue. The prologue introduces the theme and setting of the play. It provides a context for understanding the scenes that follow. What a prologue is to a drama, Genesis 1—11 is to the Bible. It provides the essential background for understanding God's saving activity.

In chapters 1—11 of Genesis, we are introduced to the following themes: God is the Creator of the heavens and the earth; mankind is created in God's image; God's human creatures have sinned and lost their true destiny; civilization bears the marks of man's tragic fallenness. Against the background of these themes, we begin to understand the necessity and nature of God's saving work.

The Creation of the World

The Creator Is the Redeemer

The Bible begins with an unargued cause: God. "In the beginning God created the heavens and the earth" (Gen. 1:1). But who is this God and what is He like? In biblical faith, God is not nameless; nor is His character a matter of guesswork. Both the name and character of God are known because He has made them known.

The story of creation in Genesis was understood and interpreted by Israel in the light of her redemption in the Exodus. First, God chose Israel to be His people. The choice was not based on Israel's goodness but on God's sovereign love. He redeemed the people from Egypt and made a covenant with them. He led them, provided for their needs, disciplined them, and worked through them for His saving purpose. In this covenant relationship, Israel came to know Him as the Lord of history, the Sovereign of the nations, and the God of redeeming love. They believed in God as Creator because, in their own history, they knew His creative and redemptive power.

From the experience of redemption, Israel looked back on the beginning of all things. No explanation of origins was adequate apart from the God they knew in the Exodus and the covenant. Creation, therefore, could not be the result of chance. Nor could the Creator of the heavens and the earth be a blind, impersonal force. Rather, the Creator was none other than the Lord of history, the loving Redeemer of His people.

Creation Is Purposive

Because God always acts in meaningful ways, creation cannot be understood as an accident. It was not the result of a haphazard combination of elements. The world *is* because God *willed* it to be.

The purposive nature of God's creative work is seen in the emphasis put on His *word*. In Genesis 1 it is impressive to see how the whole creation story is determined by the *word* of God. Ten times in this chapter the phrase "and God said" occurs (vv. 3,6,9,11,14,20,24, 26,28-29).

Creation by the word of God is a recurring theme in the Bible. The psalmist declared, "By the word of the Lord were the heavens made, their starry host by the breath of his mouth. For he spoke, and it came to be; he commanded, and it stood firm" (Ps. 33:6,9). Again he wrote, "Praise him, sun and moon, praise him, all you shining stars. Praise him, you highest heavens and you waters above the skies. Let them praise the name of the Lord, for he commanded and they were created" (Ps. 148:3-5).

The same theme is prominent in the New Testament. The author of Hebrews affirmed, "By faith we understand that the world was created by the word of God, so that what is seen was made out of things which do not appear" (11:3, RSV). In John's Gospel, we read, "In the beginning was the Word, and the Word was with God, and the Word was God. He was with God in the beginning. Through him all things were made; without him nothing was made that has been made" (1:1-3). These words have often been referred to as a New Testament commentary on the first chapter of Genesis.

The verb "create" *(bara)* is special in the Old Testament. It always has God as its subject; it is never used of human activity. Many scholars believe that the verb implies that God created the world "out of nothing" *(ex nihilo)*. God's creativity is unique. Creation, therefore, has a quality that is different from anything made by human hands. Of this uniqueness, a New Testament writer observed: "By faith we understand that the universe was formed at God's command, so that what is seen was not made out of what was visible" (Heb. 11:3).

A human artist or craftsman does not create out of nothing. He gives form to materials that are already at hand whether wood, stone, clay, or paints and canvas. He is bound by the limitations of the materials he uses. The materials set limits to the freedom of the craftsman. But God did not make the world from material that was already at hand. He created out of nothing. The very elements which constitute our world were brought into being by God.

To say that God made all things out of nothing means that there is no eternal reality alongside of God. No power rivals His power. The world depends on God for its existence; He does not depend on it. God is the transcendent Lord over all creation. He is the One who declared: "I am the Lord, who has made all things, who alone stretched out the heavens, who spread out the earth by myself" (Isa. 44:24; see Ps. 102:25; Job 38:4-11).

Creation Is Good

A recurring refrain in Genesis 1 is "and God saw that it was good" (vv. 10,12,18,21,25). The statement at the end of the chapter is even more emphatic: "And God saw everything that he had made, and behold, it was very good" (v. 31, RSV).

The world is good because it was created by the good God. Unlike some religions, biblical faith is world affirming rather than world denying. There is nothing inherently evil in the material creation. This Old Testament insight is confirmed by the New Testament. Against a legalistic, world-denying attitude Paul wrote, "For everything created by God is good, and nothing is to be rejected if it is received with thanksgiving" (1 Tim. 4:4, RSV). The world, therefore, is to be received as God's good gift.

Creation of Mankind

Mankind, like the material world, is God's creation. The same special word which is used in Genesis 1:1 of the heavens and the earth is used in 1:27 to affirm that God created the human species. Neither the universe nor man resulted from chance. Both came into being as a result of God's willful activity.

Finite but Free

The creation of human life is described in a picturesque way in Genesis 2:7. "Then the Lord God formed man of dust from the ground, and breathed into his nostrils the breath of life; and man became a living being" (RSV) The verb "formed" in this verse is the word used of a potter forming clay into a usable vessel (Jer. 1:1-18). That God forms man from dust is a reminder that human life is creaturely and finite. Man does not have life from himself but from God. Man is neither divine nor a spark of the divine. He has life only because God chooses to give it. There is, therefore, no basis for pride.

Though finite and dependent, human beings are free. Freedom means the ability to act in accordance with one's own purpose and intent. God did not create robots who respond automatically to prearranged signals. Nor should we think of humans as puppets to be manipulated by God apart from their will. God gave to this unique species the awesome gift of freedom. Only in this context does responsibility have any meaning. The decision to love God or to rebel against Him is the result of a real choice.

Freedom Within Limits

Though freedom is real, God established the boundaries within which freedom is to be exercised. "The Lord God commanded the man, 'You are free to eat from any tree in the garden; but you must not eat from the tree of the knowledge of good and evil, for when you eat of it you will surely die'" (Gen. 2:16-17). What was the reason for such a limitation? John Calvin suggested that it was "not because God would have him to stray like a sheep, without judgment and without choice; but that he might not seek to be wiser than became him, nor by trusting to his own understanding, cast off the yoke of God, and constitute himself an arbiter and judge of good and evil."[1]

Only God knows what is good and not good. To seek to know good and evil apart from God is to establish one's own righteousness rather than to receive the righteousness that comes from God (see Rom. 10:2-4). It is a use of freedom that goes beyond the boundary which God established. Such misuse of freedom is to defy God, and it incurs the warning, "You shall die" (Gen. 2:17, RSV).

Created in God's Image

"Then God said, 'Let us make man in our image, after our likeness'; . . . . So God created man in his own image, in the image of God he created him; male and female he created them" (Gen. 1:26-27, RSV). No other verses in the Old Testament describe so truly the uniqueness of human beings. But what does it mean to be created in God's image and likeness?

First, it should be noted that "in our image" and "after our likeness" mean the same thing. This is an example of Hebrew parallelism. One phrase reinforces the other. The meaning is that human beings are made "in God's image, that is to say, in his likeness."[2]

Furthermore, *one aspect* of man should not be isolated and identified as the image. For example, some people identify the image as the intellect. Certainly the ability to reason is part of our uniqueness. But is it sufficient by itself? Others define image as the ability to make moral decisions. This includes our rational capacity but is a broader category. Still others identify the image as something spiritual in human nature, such as spirit or soul. Attempts to limit the image in these ways have not been satisfactory. Whatever the image is, it involves the whole person.

The meaning of the image.—A helpful approach is to understand the image as the capacity for a personal relationship with God. We are *relational beings*. We are created for a relationship of loving trust in and faithful obedience to our Creator. Only in this right relationship with God do we fulfill our highest purpose as creatures. More than anything else, this capacity sets us apart from the rest of creation. We can hear God's word and make a conscious and deliberate response to Him. This includes reason and the ability to make moral decisions but is more comprehensive. It involves the total person.

The implications of this view are seen clearly in the following statement:

> All the rest of the creation obeys God's will without conscious volition: the stars in their courses mechanically complete their appointed liturgy; even the animals by instinct fulfill the law of their creation. To man alone is given the responsibility of conscious choice; man alone is free to disobey the Creator's will. Thus it is that man alone is conscious of his responsibility before God, is aware that he stands in the presence and under the judgment of God.[3]

The nature of the image as relational is also seen in God's creation of man as male and female. "Male and female" (Gen. 1:27) indicates that man is not man alone. Vertically, man is created to relate to God in fellowship. Horizontally, man is created for relationships with other human beings. Individuals find their greatest fulfillment in community. Human life is, therefore, both individual and social.

The image and man's stewardship.—As a consequence of being created in God's image, man is to rule over the earth. The decision to create man in the divine image is followed by the words: "Let them rule over the fish of the sea and the birds of the air, over the livestock, over all the earth, and over all the creatures that move along the ground" (Gen. 1:26; compare 1:28; 2:15,19-20).

Psalm 8 has been called a commentary on Genesis 1:26. There, too, man's unique status has been linked with his rule of the earth.

> You made him a little lower than the
> heavenly beings
> and crowned him with glory and
> honor.
>
> You made him ruler over the works of
> your hands;
> you put everything under his feet:
> all flocks and herds,
> and the beasts of the field,
> the birds of the air

and the fish of the sea,
all that swim the paths of the seas
(vv. 5-8).

Under God the care of the earth is man's responsibility. He is to use the resources of the world in a wise and creative way. Creation is to be enjoyed, but not selfishly exploited. It is to be used, but not wasted. The authority to rule is delegated to man by God. It is, therefore, a stewardship for which one is responsible to God.

Sin and the Fall

The Problem of Sin's Origin

An age-old question that still haunts thoughtful people is, Where did sin come from? Though volumes have been written on the subject, no one can solve all the problems. The biblical writers were deeply concerned about the reality of sin. They did not, however, speculate about its origin. They were more concerned with the tragic effects of sin in the lives of individuals and society. Most of their attention was focused on God's response to and victory over sin.

One thing is certain. Nowhere does the Bible suggest that God is the author of sin. Such an idea would be blasphemous. It would contradict the holiness of God. In the New Testament, James recognized how inconceivable it would be to think of God tempting one to sin. "When tempted, no one should say, 'God is tempting me.' For God cannot be tempted by evil, nor does he tempt anyone" (Jas. 1:13). There is nothing in God to which sin can make its appeal. If God is so completely free from sin, then it is impossible to think that He would cause it in someone else.

Temptation came to Adam and Eve from a source outside themselves. It came neither from God nor from a source existing eternally alongside God. Surprisingly the temptation came from one of God's creatures. "Now the serpent was more crafty than any of the wild animals that the Lord God had made" (Gen. 3:1).

In many ancient religions, the serpent is a symbol of evil. Old Testament writers often used the serpent figure to depict evil men or nations (Deut. 32:33; Pss. 58:4; 140:3; Isa. 14:29; Jer. 8:17). Sometimes it represents evil or danger in general (Ps. 91:13). In Revelation 12:9 "that ancient serpent" is identified as "the devil or Satan" (compare Rev. 20:2). This identification is not made explicitly in Genesis 3. Attention is focused more on the crafty nature of the creature and the cunning way temptation was presented.

The responsibility for the reality of sin in the world must finally rest with man. Though tempted from without, man was not overwhelmed against his will. He was free to choose. The Bible never allows human beings to blame their sin on either circumstances or other persons. One may protest, "But I couldn't help it!" or "I was a victim of a bad situation!" or even worse, "The devil made me do it!" Such protests have a hollow ring in light of the Bible's emphasis on personal responsibility. Such responsibility is assumed rather than argued in Genesis 3. It was affirmed by the prophet: "The soul who sins is the one who will die. . . . The righteousness of the righteous man will be credited to him, and the wickedness of the wicked will be charged against him" (Ezek. 18:20). It was reinforced by Paul: "So then, each of us will give an account of himself to God" (Rom. 14:12).

The Method of Temptation

God's goodness was questioned.—The serpent asked, "Did God really say, 'You must not eat from any tree in the garden'?" (Gen. 3:1). The question was designed to create doubts about the goodness of God. The serpent implied that God was selfish and that He was being unfair by placing limitations on His creatures.

Eve answered the question with no and yes. No, God did not forbid eating from all the trees; but yes, God did forbid eating from one tree. The serpent's question twisted God's command in 2:17. It planted the seed of doubt. "What was God's *real* motive in keeping you from the knowledge of good and evil?"

When Eve answered, she exaggerated God's command by adding the phrase "neither shall you touch it" (Gen. 3:3, RSV). This overstatement may indicate her growing resentment at the restriction. It is as if she said, "We can't even touch the tree which is in the midst of the garden."

God's truthfulness was denied.—The statement, "You will not surely die" (Gen. 3:4) denied the truth of God's warning. The integrity of God was assailed. Not only that, but "God knows that when you eat of it your eyes will be opened, and you will be like God, knowing good and evil" (v. 5). The suggestion was that God did not tell the truth about the limitations He placed on His creatures. His concern was not for their good but for His own selfish reasons.

Sin was made desirable.—When Eve "saw that the fruit of the tree was good for food and pleasing to the eye, and also desirable for gaining wisdom, she took some and ate it" (Gen. 3:6). Temptation is deceptive. It comes in the guise of satisfying three normal desires: food, beauty, and wisdom. There is a legitimate way of satisfying these desires. They may be rightfully fulfilled within the will of God. Apart from God's will, however, these desires degenerate into "the lust of the flesh and the lust of the eyes and the pride of life" (1 John 2:16, RSV). Listening to the cunning creature rather than the Creator, Adam and Eve crossed the boundary from life to death.

The Nature of Sin

Sin is against God.—Sin is primarily a religious reality. It can be understood properly when it is seen as against God. W. T. Conner expressed it in this way: "Crime is against the state. Immorality is against society. But, sin is against God."[4] He did not mean that crime and immorality were not also sin. But they could be classified as sin only because they are also against God. This means that the standard for determining what is sinful is God's nature. Anything that is inconsistent with God's nature and purpose is sinful. If there were no God, sin would have no meaning. Ultimately, sin is what it is because God is who He is. There are several illustrations of this in the Bible.

When Joseph was tempted by Potiphar's wife, his response was, "How then could I do such a wicked thing and sin against God?" (Gen. 39:9). To have yielded would have been a violation of his master's trust as well as a wrong against his wife. But what made it sinful was that it was against God.

The psalmist cried to God, "For I know my transgressions, and my sin is ever before me. Against you, you only, have I sinned and done what is evil in your sight" (Ps. 51:4). Whatever the effects of his sin on himself and other people, his transgressions were sinful because they were against God.

A vision of God's nature as holy had a similar effect on Isaiah. "Woe is me!" he lamented. "I am ruined! For I am a man of unclean lips, and I live among a people of unclean lips and my eyes have seen the King, the Lord Almighty" (Isa. 6:5). Only in the light of God's nature could the prophet see the truth of his sinfulness and the uncleanness of his people.

Sin as unbelief.—Temptation gained a foothold when Adam and Eve doubted the integrity of God. Moving from doubt to unbelief required only a small step.

In this context, unbelief does not mean to deny the existence of God but to reject His lordship. One may argue that there is a God and still refuse to believe in Him. The tragedy of unbelief is that man no longer accepts God as the source of all goodness and truth. God's claims are rejected and replaced with the illusion of self-sufficiency. Decisions are made without reference to the will of God. Unbelief is not just an occasional act. It is an attitude and way of life. It is the companion of disobedience (Num. 14:11; 20:12; Ps. 78:22; Isa. 7:9).

The implications of unbelief are expressed clearly in John's writings. Not to believe is to live under condemnation (John 3:18), to be cut off from eternal life and subject to God's wrath (v. 36). Furthermore, to refuse to believe is to treat God as a liar (1 John 5:10). One of the functions of the Holy Spirit is to convince the world that it is a sin not to believe in God's revelation in Jesus (John 16:9).

Sin as rebellion.—Rebellion involves resistance to authority and opposition to control. When Adam and Eve sinned, they defied the lordship of God and sought to usurp authority for themselves.

This is an essential element in the biblical view of sin. When the prophets scolded Israel, this was the decisive note. For example, "Hear, O heavens! Listen, O earth! For the Lord has spoken: 'I reared children and brought them up, but they have rebelled against me. The ox knows his master, the donkey his owner's manger, but Israel does not know, my people do not understand'" (Isa. 1:2-3). Or again, "Son of man, I am sending you to the Israelites, to a rebellious nation that has rebelled against me . . . to this very day" (Ezek. 2:3). In Jesus' parable of the laborers in the vineyard (Mark 12:1-12), the laborers rebelled against the owner's authority. They withheld the profits, mistreated his servants, and killed his son.

Sin as pride.—The appeal to pride is evident in the serpent's deceptive promise: "You will be like God" (Gen. 3:5). Here is the lure of being free from God and of deciding for oneself what is best for life.

Pride is the centering of attention on self rather than on God. In pride the creature seeks to take the Creator's place at the center of one's own existence and to become the master of one's own destiny. Pride is the seed that grows into many other sins, such as cruelty, tyranny, greed, self-righteousness, and insensitivity to God and other people. A vivid description of pride and its relation to unbelief and idolatry is found in the Epistle to the Romans:

> What may be known about God is plain to them, because God has made it plain to them. For since the creation of the world God's invisible qualities—his eternal power and divine nature—have been clearly seen, being understood from what has been made, so that men are without excuse. *Although they claimed to be wise, they became fools and exchanged the glory of the immortal God for images made to look like mortal man and birds and animals and reptiles* (Rom. 1:19-20,22-23, author's italics).

Many Christians, ancient and modern, have described pride as the essence of sin. Augustine taught that all sin begins in pride. He defined pride as undue exaltation. "Now, exaltation is inordinate when the soul cuts itself off from the very Source to which it should keep close and somehow makes itself and becomes an end to itself."[5] C. S. Lewis labeled pride as "the great sin." "It was through pride that the devil became the devil: Pride leads to every other vice: it is the complete anti-God state of mind."[6]

The Effects of Sin

Fellowship with God is broken.—When Adam and Eve sinned, "they hid from the Lord God among the trees of the garden" (Gen. 3:8). They lost the free and open communion they had had with God. The tragedy of this loss is seen when we remember that we were created for fellowship with God. To be separated from God is to be cut off from the purpose of life. God created us for a relationship of trust and obedience with Him. To rebel against God and to break this relationship with Him is to be lost. The very nature of sin is to alienate a person from God. Sin shuts God out of one's life. Isaiah diagnosed it correctly: "But your iniquities have separated you from God; your sins have hidden his face from you, so that he will not hear" (Isa. 59:2).

Fellowship with one another is broken.—When our relationship with God is broken, our relationship with other persons is also affected. The first impulse of Adam, when confronted with the reality of his sin, was to blame Eve (Gen. 3:12). The relationship between man and woman was not the same after sin as it was before. Adam's joy at seeing Eve for the first time (Gen. 2:23) gave way to resentment.

Guilt is experienced.—The words "I was afraid because I was naked, so I hid" (Gen. 3:10) indicated that the first couple had been in a state of innocence. They experienced no shame. But their sin changed this. The shame that engulfed them was evidence of their guilt.

Guilt, however, is more than a subjective sense of shame. A person may or may not feel guilty. It is also possible for a person to feel guilty for no valid reason. Theologically, guilt is much deeper than feeling ashamed. It refers to one's status before God. Guilt is the state of one who has sinned before God and is thus liable to punishment. In this sense, a person can be guilty whether he feels guilty or not (compare Rom. 3:10; Jas. 2:10).

The image of God is marred.—This is not stated in so many words, but it is implied in the continuing history of mankind. The image of God is man's capacity for fellowship with God. It is the ability to know and to love God in a relationship of personal communion. But this communion has been disrupted. Man no longer serves God nor loves Him as he should.

Is it still possible to speak of God's image in man? Or has the image been completely destroyed? It is more accurate to say that the image has been marred or twisted rather than wiped out altogether. In Genesis 9:6 shedding a person's blood is forbidden "for in the image of

God has God made man." Cursing others with the tongue is prohibited because they "have been made in God's likeness" (Jas. 3:9). But if the image is still present, it is only a broken relic of the original. Man himself cannot restore it. It remains broken until it is renewed by the One who is the perfect image of God.

Death becomes a reality.—The presence of the tree of the knowledge of good and evil was accompanied by a warning: "In the day that you eat from it you shall surely die" (Gen. 2:17, NASB). The fact that Adam and Eve did not die physically in that moment does not mean that the warning was annulled. There is more than one way to die!

Death in the Bible is more than a biological reality. There is a spiritual death which is the result of separation from God. This is described as being "dead in trespasses and sins" (Eph. 2:1, KJV) because "separated from the life of God" (Eph. 4:18). Death as the wages of sin is contrasted with eternal life which is God's gift (Rom. 6:23). Furthermore, "The mind of sinful man is death, but the mind controlled by the Spirit is life and peace" (Rom. 8:6). And, "Anyone who does not love remains in death" (1 John 3:14). Sin consigns us to a life of death now and threatens us with eternal separation from God which is "the second death" (Rev. 21:8).

What, then, is the status of physical death? Is it simply a biological necessity with no relation to sin? Not necessarily! Paul referred to physical death when he spoke of the universal reign of death which entered the world through Adam's sin (Rom. 5:12). In 1 Corinthians 15 the resurrection of Christ is portrayed as a victory over physical death. Since an essential part of God's saving activity is to overcome death, physical death may be included as one of the consequences of sin.[7]

Human nature is depraved.—Depravity means that human nature has become twisted to the point that one can no longer relate rightly to God, self, or others. Sin is not something external; it is more like a disease that has distorted the center of personality. Theologians often refer to this condition as *total depravity*. The phrase is valid so long as it is not misused. Total depravity does not mean that a person is so completely evil that he is not capable of any good. Some good deeds are possible from the worst of people. People do differ in their standards of morality and degree of moral achievement. There is a considerable difference between Adolf Hitler on the one hand and Albert Schweitzer on the other. If this were not so, then all of our moral comparisons would be meaningless.

The point of total depravity is that sin has affected the whole person. No aspect of human personality (reason, emotions, will, body) has escaped its effects. Two implications emerge from this fact. First, even the good we do is often tainted by self-interest. Second, this sinful condition is a trap from which we cannot free ourselves no matter how heroic the effort.

Curse on the processes of nature.—The joyful prospect of having children was overshadowed by the prospect of travail and sorrow (Gen. 3:16). In Genesis 1:28 the increase of the human race was the result of divine blessing, but it passed under the shadow of fallenness.

The close union between man and the ground was also affected. Of itself, the earth produced "thorns and thistles" (v. 18). Only by laborious toil can the earth be made to yield the food needed for human survival. This does not mean that work itself is a curse. But because of sin that work involves drudgery and frustration.

The sad conclusion to Genesis 3 is the expulsion of Adam and Eve from Eden. Created to know and love God, to reflect His glory and to rule the earth in His name, they were thrust out of their earthly paradise. No amount of sorrow, seeking, or effort could restore the loss. God placed "cherubim and a flaming sword flashing back and forth to guard the way to the tree of life" (v. 24).

The Continuing Consequences of the Fall

Cain and Abel

If one is not right with God, one cannot be right anywhere. So the sin that perverts one's relations with God perverts relations with others and with the whole creation. The truth of this is painfully evident in history following the expulsion from the garden.

The story of Cain and Abel illustrates the effects of sin in human relationships. In a fit of jealousy over the rejection of his offering in favor of Abel's, Cain killed his brother (Gen. 4:3-8). Why one offering was acceptable and the other was not is not stated. A probable clue is to be found in the attitude of the two men. "By faith Abel offered a more acceptable sacrifice than Cain" (Heb. 11:4). Cain's actions throughout the story are evidence of his rebellious attitude (Gen. 4:6). In biblical religion, the spirit of the worshiper is more important than the offering itself (compare Prov. 15:8; Mic. 6:6-8).

God sought out the rebellious Cain and gave him a chance to admit guilt and receive forgiveness. To God's question, "Where is Abel, your brother?" Cain lied, "I do not know . . . Am I my brother's keeper?" (Gen. 4:9). That one is responsible for others is part of God's purpose. Responsibility to God involves responsibility for others. Service to God means serving one another. Love for God implies love for one's neighbor. Cain repudiated this kind of responsibility. Thus, as Adam was driven out of Eden, so Cain was sent as a wanderer to the land of Nod, east of Eden (v. 16).

Early Civilization

Genesis 4:17-24 gives a fleeting glimpse of early civilization through the line of Cain. We can see that the development of civilization was not the cure for sin. Rather, man's sin had a corrupting effect. Advancement in culture was not advancement toward God. Progress in society was and still is progress accompanied by sin. Sinful man always carries his sin with him.

The Flood

These chapters in Genesis illustrate the malignant growth of sin. "The Lord saw how great man's wickedness on the earth had become, and that every inclination of the thoughts of his heart was only evil all the time. The Lord was grieved that he had made man on the earth, and his heart was filled with pain" (Gen. 6:5-6).

Though Noah found favor with God, the rest of mankind had become corrupt indeed. In Genesis 6:11-12, the word "corrupt" is used three times to describe the human condition. This chapter stands in stark contrast to Genesis 1. In the earlier chapter, God saw what He created and declared that it was good. In this chapter, the Lord saw "how great man's wickedness on the earth had become."

The story of the Flood not only tells about the corruption of mankind but also speaks about God's nature. God loves His creatures. But His love is not an easygoing sentimentalism. God does not tolerate rebellion. Sin is always met by divine judgment.

The Tower of Babel

Not even the Flood, however, could quell human pride. The people who congregated on the plain of Shinar decided to build a city "with a tower that reaches to the heavens, so that we may make a name for ourselves, and not be scattered over the face of the whole earth" (Gen. 11:4). Their efforts were motivated by their pride rather than by submission to God. They were more concerned to make a name for themselves than to glorify the name of God.

There is a certain irony in the story. The tower was to be so big that it would reach the heavens. But in reality it was so small that God had to "come . . . down" (v. 7) to see it. In judgment God confused their language and "scattered them over the face of the whole earth" (v. 9).

Confusion of languages is a vivid symbol of the barriers that exist between people. The problems of communication between people are deeper than difficulties in translation. The fear and hostility among the nations of the world have a moral and spiritual basis. Sin, especially when seen as pride, is responsible for the hostile walls that separate people from one another. The different languages and cultures are only external manifestations. The barriers between nations reflect the judgment of God and the inevitable effects of sin on all human relationships.

The tragic story of sin and its consequences does not end with Genesis 1—11. These chapters tell of the beginning of sin in the history of the race. They also mirror the experience of humanity in each succeeding generation. Standing in the shadow of fallenness, each person repeats in his own experience the Adam type of sin. At this fundamental point, there is no difference between people "for all have sinned and fall short of the glory of God" (Rom. 3:23). "Therefore, just as sin entered the world through one man, and death through sin, and in this way death came to all men, because all sinned" (Rom. 5:12). Both Old and New Testament, as well as human experience in every age, confirm Paul's indictment of all humanity in Romans 1:18-32 and 3:10-18.

Glimpses of Grace

The story of sin, however, is not the only story. It is not even the most important story. Of far greater importance is the story of God's graciousness. Even in the early chapters of Genesis, there are glimpses of that graciousness.

Genesis 3:15 has been called the *protoevangelium* or first gospel. Speaking to the serpent, God promised, "I will put enmity between you and the woman, and between your offspring and hers: he will crush your head, and you will strike his heel." This verse portrays the continuing conflict between the woman and the serpent and between their descendants. This hostility would have a twofold effect. The serpent's head would be bruised by the woman's offspring and the woman's offspring would be wounded by the serpent. This is not a messianic prophecy in the explicit sense. But many Christians believe that it is messianic in principle. If so, then it is a picture of the conflict which was climaxed on the cross. Ultimately Christ has crushed the head of the serpent-tempter.

Genesis 3:21 also shows God's mercy. God clothed the nakedness of Adam and Eve, enabling them to live with their shame. In spite of what they had done, God cared for them.

Cain, too, experienced God's mercy. He complained that his punishment was greater than he could bear (Gen. 4:13). In response God voiced a sevenfold vengeance on anyone who killed Cain. God also put a mark on him to make this protective relationship evident to all.

Genesis 8:21 and following is another glimpse into the heart of God. The Flood was the result of God's judgment and His determination to make a new start. But the new beginning does not take place in a new paradise, but in a world already marked by fallenness. In spite of human sin, however, God will uphold the natural orders necessary for man's life in the world. The rainbow is a sign of both God's promise and man's hope.

God's grace would become clearer in the call of Abraham and the covenant with Israel. It would be clearest of all in Jesus Christ.

Notes

1. Quoted by Henri Blocher, *In the Beginning: The Opening Chapters of Genesis,* trans. David G. Pearson, p. 133.
2. Alan Richardson, *Genesis 1-11, Torch Bible Commentaries,* p. 54.
3. Ibid.
4. Walter T. Conner, *The Gospel of Redemption,* p. 1.
5. Augustine, *The City of God,* trans. Gerald G. Walsh, Demetrius B. Zema, Grace Monahan, and Daniel J. Honan; ed. and abridged Vernon J. Bourke (Garden City, New York: Doubleday & Co., Inc., 1958), p. 309.
6. C. S. Lewis, *Mere Christianity,* rev. ed. (New York: Macmillan Publishing Co., 1960), p. 109.
7. For a discussion see Leon Morris, *The Wages of Sin* (London: The Tyndale Press, 1954).

Bibliography

Blocher, Henri. *In the Beginning: The Opening Chapters of Genesis*. Translated by David G. Pearson. Downers Grove, Illinois: Inter-Varsity Press, 1984.

Boice, James Montgomery. *Genesis: An Expositional Commentary, Vol. 1 Genesis 1:1 to 11:32*. Grand Rapids: The Zondervan Corp., 1982.

Conner, Walter T. *The Gospel of Redemption*. Nashville: Broadman Press, 1945.

Francisco, Clyde T. *Genesis. The Broadman Bible Commentary,* 1, Revised. Edited by Clifton J. Allen. Nashville: Broadman Press, 1969.

Fretheim, Terence E. *Creation, Fall and Flood: Studies in Genesis 1—11*. Minneapolis: Augsburg Publishing House, 1969.

Fritsch, Charles T. *Genesis. The Layman Bible Commentary,* 2. Edited by Balmer H. Kelly. Richmond: John Knox Press, 1959.

Houston, James M. *I Believe in the Creator*. Grand Rapids: William B. Eerdmans Publishing Co., 1980.

Kidner, Derek. *Genesis. Tyndale Old Testament Commentaries*. Edited by D. J. Wiseman. Downers Grove, Illinois: Inter-Varsity Press, 1967.

Marshall, I. Howard. *Pocket Guide to Christian Beliefs*. Downers Grove, Illinois: Inter-Varsity Press, 1978.

Richardson, Alan. *Genesis 1—11. Torch Bible Commentaries*. London: SCM Press, Ltd., 1953.

Thielicke, Helmut. *How the World Began: Man in the First Chapters of the Bible*. Translated by John W. Doberstein. Philadelphia: The Muhlenberg Press, 1961.

Youngblood, Ronald. *How It All Began: Genesis 1—11*. Ventura, California: Regal Books, 1980.

2

The Promise of Salvation

If God commissioned us to deal with the world's rebellion, what would we do? What kind of scheme would we devise? What course of action would we follow? An unknown poet pondered these questions and wrote,

> If I were God
> And man made a mire
> Of things: war, hatred,
> Murder, lust, cobwebs,
> Of infamy, entangling
> The heart and soul
> I would sweep him
> To one side and start anew.
> (I think I would.)
> If I did this,
> Would I be God?[1]

Fortunately God did not sweep man to one side and start anew. He sought to save rather than to destroy. Genesis 1—11 tells the story of man's rebellious flight from God. The rest of the Bible is the story of God's loving pursuit of man.

The Call of Abraham

God began with one man in Ur of the Chaldees. To Abraham came the divine command: "Leave your country, your people and your father's household and go to the land I will show you" (Gen. 12:1). This event is evidence that God had not abandoned His world. It heralds the divine initiative in dealing with human rebellion and restoring mankind to fellowship with Himself.

The Beginning of Salvation History

The call of Abraham is the first link in what is called *salvation history*. Salvation history refers to that series of events in the life and history of Israel which led to the coming of Jesus Christ the Savior. It is the story of God's saving activity to which the Old and New Testaments bear witness. To speak of salvation history does not imply that history itself saves. Rather, it means that God has acted in a particular series of world events to accomplish His redemptive purpose. God alone saves, but history is the arena in which He works out His goals. Genesis 12:1-3, therefore, portrays the divine response to the rebellion described in Genesis 11. It is the link between Genesis 1—11 and the rest of the Bible.

The Covenant Relationship

It involved a promise.—God's promise to Abraham is revealed in these words: "I will make you into a great nation and I will bless you; I will make your name great, and you will be a blessing. I will bless those who bless you, and whoever curses you I will curse; and all peoples on earth will be blessed through you" (Gen. 12:2-3). The promise is repeated in Genesis 15 and 17. Three elements are involved. God vowed to give Abraham a son who would be the heir to the promise, to give him numerous descendants, and to give him the land in which he sojourned.

To confirm the promise, God entered into a covenant with Abraham. A covenant is a special relationship initiated by God with an individual or nation. It is not a contract between equals. Then, as now, God is always the initiator and He always remains sovereign in the relationship. God's covenant begins in His grace, and it is a pledge of His faithfulness. By accepting this relationship, Abraham agreed to the responsibilities which went with it.

The covenant was sealed by a solemn ceremony (Gen. 15:8-11). In ancient times, two parties to an agreement killed one or more animals and cut their carcasses into halves. The halves were placed opposite each other and the two parties walked between them. This symbolized their mutual agreement. It also suggested that if one of them broke the covenant, he should be slain like the animals (compare Jer. 34:18).

It involved a purpose.—God's purpose in calling Abraham must be kept clear. His ultimate reason involved sending His own Son into the world for the salvation of humanity. The call of Abraham was for the purpose of preparing a people through whom God's Son would come. God's choice of one person was for the blessing of the many: "All peoples on earth will be blessed through you" (Gen. 12:3). The whole story of God's saving activity is implicit in the covenant with Abraham. It is not by accident, therefore, that New Testament writers trace the genealogy of Jesus back through David to Abraham (Matt. 1:1) and see in Jesus' coming the fruition of this ancient promise (Luke 1:72-73).

The Divine Election

The questions often arise, But why Abraham? Was there something special about him? Why not choose someone else? Why begin with just one person? From a human point of view, it may not look like a very hopeful start. As we read the biblical story, however, we become aware that God has His own way of doing things. More than once His activity will remind us of His words: " 'For my thoughts are not your thoughts, neither are your ways my ways,' declares the Lord. 'As the heavens are higher than the earth, so are my ways higher than your ways and my thoughts than your thoughts' " (Isa. 55:8-9). Finally the choice of one man, Abraham, was a matter of divine election.[2]

Some people feel uncomfortable with the subject of election. It seems to make God arbitrary and unfair. Election is thought to imply favoritism and to foster pride. Is such a concept really consistent with the biblical message that God loves the whole world?

Properly understood, election originates in God's sovereign love. It is not based on human merit. Thus the choice of Abraham is not to be understood as a reward for good conduct. Far from fostering pride, it promotes humility.

In the Bible, election is primarily a call to service. God chose people and nations in order to achieve His purpose through them. God called Abraham so that through him "all peoples on earth will be blessed" (Gen. 12:3). One so chosen was obligated to be faithful to the divine purpose. If responsibility were sacrificed for privilege, serious consequences followed. Amos put it this way: "You only have I chosen of all the families of the earth; therefore I will punish you for all your sins" (Amos 3:2). Centuries after Abraham, Jesus reflected on this obligation: "From everyone who has been given much, much will be demanded; and from the one who has been entrusted with much, much more will be asked" (Luke 12:48).

Abraham's Faithful Response

The Old Testament summarizes Abraham's response to the divine call in one verse: "Abraham believed the Lord; and he credited it to him as righteousness" (Gen. 15:6; compare Rom. 4:3). "Believe" here means trusting God's word. It is the conviction that God will do what He promised even if it seems humanly impossible. Even so, Abraham's faith did not mature without struggle. It was a faith tempered in the fires of crisis.

The divine command.—Abraham's supreme crisis came from God Himself. After the birth of Isaac, God commanded, "Take your son, your only son Isaac, whom you love, and go to the region of Moriah. Sacrifice him there as a burnt offering on one of the mountains I will tell you about" (Gen. 22:2). Can you imagine how this sounded to Abraham? Did he misunderstand God's word to him? Did God really expect him to do this terrible deed? Surely there must be some mistake! It is difficult to imagine a more painful test for a parent's faith.

Much more than natural affection was involved in this crisis. God's own faithfulness was also on trial. God had promised that through Abraham's seed blessing would extend to all nations of the earth. Isaac was the child of that promise, the tangible evidence of divine faithfulness. In fact, Isaac was born after Abraham and Sarah had passed the normal age for having children (Gen. 18:11; compare Heb. 11:11-12). And now the promise was threatened by God's strange command.

The divine provision.—Nevertheless, Abraham obeyed. He refused to put a limit on his faith in God. To Isaac's searching question, "The fire and the wood are here but where is the lamb for the burnt offering?" Abraham replied, "God himself will provide the lamb for the burnt offering, my son" (Gen. 22:7-8). And God did provide! At the last moment, Abraham was stopped by an angel of the Lord: "'Do not lay a hand on the boy,' he said. 'Do not do anything to him. Now I know that you fear God, because you have not withheld from me your son, your only son'" (v. 12). Abraham saw a ram caught in a thicket and offered it in place of Isaac. "So Abraham called that place, 'The Lord will provide'" (v. 14).

Looking back on this event, we know that Abraham's trust was what God wanted rather than the life of his son. It is easy to understand, however, why Christians have seen in this event a parallel to the sacrifice of Christ on the cross. Abraham's son was spared, but God "did not spare his own Son, but gave him up for us all" (Rom. 8:32).

The Deliverance of Israel

To overestimate the importance of the Exodus from Egypt would be difficult. Few events have had such far-reaching effects on history and faith. This event lies at the very heart of the Old Testament. By this act, a group of slaves was delivered from bondage. In the covenant established at Sinai, they began to be a nation. Through the history of this nation in the Old Testament, we can trace the movement of God's saving activity.

Numerous references in the Old Testament confirm the central place of the Exodus in Israel's faith. Deuteronomy 6:20-23 is typical:

> In the future, when your son asks you, "What is the meaning of these stipulations, decrees and laws the Lord our God has commanded you?" tell him: "We were slaves of Pharaoh in Egypt, but the Lord brought us out of Egypt with a mighty hand. Before our eyes the Lord sent miraculous signs and wonders—great and terrible—upon Egypt and Pharaoh and his whole household. But he brought us out from there to bring us in and give us the land that he promised on oath to our forefathers.

This theme is repeated in Israel's confessions (Deut. 26:8; Josh. 24:6-7; 1 Sam. 12:6), celebrated by her poets (Pss. 77,78,105,106,

114,135) and proclaimed by the prophets (Hos. 11:1; Amos 3:1-2; Mic. 6:3-5).

Some scholars have pointed out that the Exodus is to the Old Testament what the cross and resurrection are to the New Testament. Each event proclaims God's saving activity to people in bondage. Each anchors this divine activity in real historical events. Each involves a covenant relationship with a redeemed people and bears witness to God's lordship over nature, man, and history.[3]

God Remembers His People

The fortunes of a family.—God's promise to Abraham was repeated to his descendants, Isaac and Jacob. One of Jacob's sons, Joseph, was sold into slavery by his brothers. He was taken to Egypt where he was imprisoned for a time (Gen. 37:12-23). In the midst of his hardships, however, "the Lord was with him" (Gen. 39:21). Eventually, he was released from prison and given a prominent place in the royal administration (Gen. 41:37-40). When Egypt was threatened by a severe famine, Joseph's shrewd policies saved the country from starvation (vv. 46-57).

During the famine, Joseph's brothers went to Egypt to buy food. The brother whom they had cruelly mistreated became the instrument of their survival. Looking back on all that had happened to him, Joseph discerned the providential working of God. "Do not be angry with yourselves for selling me here, because it was to save lives that God sent me ahead of you. . . . But God sent me . . . to save your lives. . . . So then, it was not you who sent me here, but God" (Gen. 45:5-8). Shortly after this, Jacob's family moved from Canaan to Goshen and made a new beginning.

Eventually Joseph died and a new king came to power in Egypt. The new monarch "did not know about Joseph" (Ex. 1:8); therefore, he felt no obligation to the Israelites because of what Joseph had done for Egypt. In fact, the rapid growth of the Israelite population was seen as a threat by the Egyptians. As a result, a new policy was adopted in dealing with them. Slave masters were put over them "to oppress them with forced labor. . . . the Egyptians came to dread the Israelites, and worked them ruthlessly. They made their lives bitter with hard labor" (vv. 11-14). This situation lasted about four hundred years. If the Israelites remembered the covenant with Abraham, they must have wondered if God had forgotten. The best they could do under the circumstances was to groan and cry out (2:23).

The faithfulness of God.—The Israelites' cry did not fall on deaf ears. "God *heard* their groaning and he *remembered* his covenant with Abraham, with Isaac and with Jacob. So God *looked* on the Israelites and *was concerned* about them" (v. 24, author's italics). Notice the verbs in this verse! Verbs are action words. They describe the activity of the subject. As descriptions of God's activity, these verbs help us understand His nature.

The very fact that God acts tells us something important about Him. It affirms that He is personal. He is not like the gods of the nations. He is not a figment of the imagination nor a projection of human wishes. He is the living, personal God who cares for His people and responds to their distress. He acts in history to accomplish His purpose. He is known by His words and deeds.

This truth about God is the basis for the scathing denunciations of idolatry in the Old Testament. In the light of who God is, idolatry is as foolish as it is worthless. Representative of this attitude is the following:

> Why do the nations say,
>   "Where is their God?"
> Our God is in heaven;
>   he does whatever pleases him.
> But their idols are silver and gold,
>   made by the hands of men.
> They have mouths, but *cannot speak,*
>   eyes, but they *cannot see;*
> they have ears, but *cannot hear,*
>   noses, but they *cannot smell;*
> they have hands, but *cannot feel,*
>   feet, but they *cannot walk;*
>   *nor can they utter a sound* with
>   their throats.
> Those who make them will be like
>   them,

and so will all who trust in them,
(Ps. 115:2-8, author's italics; compare
Isa. 40:18-26; 45:5-7; Jer. 10:3-10).

What other gods cannot accomplish, the God of Abraham, Isaac, and Jacob can do because He is the living God.

God Chooses a Servant

God's purposes are usually achieved through the instrumentality of persons. At the beginning of the stream of salvation history, God chose Abraham. At this crucial point in the process, Moses was selected. He whom God chooses God also prepares. Moses' life is a case study in the providence of God. Eighty years were spent in getting Moses ready for his task.

Moses' early years.—God's providence is evident from the time of Moses' infancy. His life was spared in defiance of Pharaoh's command that every newborn son of the Hebrews was to be cast into the Nile (Ex. 1:15-16,22). Moses was placed by his mother in a basket which she set among the reeds on the bank of the river (Ex. 2:3; compare Heb. 11:23). He was discovered by Pharaoh's daughter who decided to adopt him in apparent defiance of her father's decree. Pharaoh's decree became the means by which the deliverer of Israel became a member of the royal household.

Also, Moses was returned to his own mother who nursed him until he was old enough to be weaned and to be adopted by the Egyptian princess. Under the guidance of his own parents, he grew into an awareness of his Hebrew identity and heritage.

Little is known about Moses' life in Pharaoh's court. The New Testament supplies only a hint. "Moses was educated in all the wisdom of the Egyptians and was powerful in speech and action" (Acts 7:22).

At some point, Moses began to identify consciously with the sufferings of the Israelites. This is evident in Moses' rash murder of an Egyptian who was beating a Hebrew (Ex. 2:11). Again the New Testament provides us with a commentary. "By faith Moses when he had grown up, refused to be known as the son of Pharaoh's daughter. He chose to be mistreated along with the people of God rather than to enjoy the pleasures of sin for a short time" (Heb. 11:24-25).

Moses' sojourn in Midian.—When the murder of the Egyptian became known, Moses fled to Midian where he spent the next forty years of his life (Ex. 2:15-25; compare Acts 7:29-30). What effect did this exile have on Moses' hope for Israel's deliverance? The Old Testament does not provide an answer to that question. Some writers suggest that Moses' marriage, raising a family, and accepting the life of a shepherd indicate that he had given up. Others believe that the name of his son, Gershom ("stranger," "alien") indicates that Moses never accepted Midian as his final destiny. Regardless of Moses' state of mind, God had neither forgotten Moses nor had He abandoned His promise.

Moses' call.—God called Moses through a bush that burned but was not consumed (Ex. 3:1-2). In this experience, God made known His plan to send Moses to Pharaoh to demand the release of His people. Two essential elements are in this call: a revelation and a commission (compare Isa. 6:1-8 for a similar pattern).

First, God revealed himself as "the God of your father, the God of Abraham, the God of Isaac and the God of Jacob" (Ex. 3:6). Moses was not asked to introduce a new God to the people but to bring a fuller revelation of the God they had known. This links all that God was about to do for Israel with His promise to Abraham. Once more, there is a strong emphasis on the divine faithfulness.

Second, God commissioned Moses. "I am sending you to Pharaoh to bring my people, the Israelites, out of Egypt" (Ex. 3:10). This must have come as a shock to Moses. He was a fugitive from justice. He had lost his standing with the Egyptians, and there is no evidence that he was respected by the Israelites. Moses' immediate reaction was to protest God's choice (Ex. 3:11 to 4:18).

To the protesting prophet, God gave two promises. The first was the promise of God's presence: "I will be with you." The second was a sign: "When you have brought the people out of Egypt, you will worship God on this mountain" (Ex. 3:12). Moses was asking for the assurance of success before he accepted the role. God was demanding that Moses go in faith. In this case, the sign would follow faith rather than precede it. The success of the mission was its own guarantee.

God Reveals His Name

In the ancient world, names often carried more significance than they do today. They were more than a convenient way of distinguishing one person from another. To know someone's name was to know his or her character. The name represented the inner reality of whoever was being named. An obvious example is the name Jacob (literally, "heel grabber" or "deceiver"). As a result of a profound spiritual experience, Jacob's name was changed to Israel ("a prince with God"). So when Moses asked for God's name, he was asking for a fuller revelation of His nature.

God's response sounds evasive. "I am who I am. This is what you are to say to the Israelites: 'I AM has sent me to you'" (Ex. 3:14). This name is composed of four letters: YHWH. These letters are part of the Hebrew verb "to be." We do not know how it was pronounced because for a long time Hebrew was written without vowels. Various translations have been suggested: "I am who I am," "I am the one who causes to be," "I will be who I will be."[4] What does it mean?

It is helpful to remember that God is known by revelation, that is, by what He does and says. With this in mind, an interpretative paraphrase might help us to understand the meaning of the name. "I am who I am in my deeds and words. If you want to know who I am, pay attention to what I do and say. I am going to deliver Israel from bondage, provide for them in the wilderness, instruct them in my ways, and use them for my purpose. In these acts you will learn the meaning of my name." Such an interpretation fits the biblical pattern that God is known by what He does. (Notice again the verbs for which God is the subject in 3:7-10.)

God Delivers His People

The plagues.—Exodus 7—12 describes a series of ten plagues which God sent on Egypt. These plagues are described as "miraculous signs and wonders" (Ex. 7:3). Such signs and wonders in the Bible were never given simply to startle or amaze people. They were not ends in themselves, rather they pointed to the activity and purpose of God. In this instance, the plagues were a sign to the pharaoh that God would free His people and that He had the power to do so. To the

Israelites, they were a sign that their deliverance would not be accomplished by any strategy of their own but by God's wisdom and might.

Some scholars have interpreted this episode as a contest between the God of Israel and the gods of Egypt as embodied in the pharaoh. If so, there was really no serious doubt about the outcome. At first Pharaoh scorned the God of Israel: "Who is the Lord, that I should obey him and let Israel go? I do not know the Lord and I will not let Israel go" (Ex. 5:2). After the tenth plague, however, Pharaoh cried: "Up! Leave my people, you and the Israelites! Go, worship the Lord as you have requested. . . . And also bless me" (Ex. 12:31-32). The impotence of the Egyptian deities to protect the most cherished possession of their people was exposed for all to see.

The Passover.—The tenth plague stands out from the others because of its severity. Moses told Pharaoh that the Lord would bring death to the firstborn son of every family in Egypt. There would be an outcry of agony such as had never been known in the land.

Special provisions were made for the Israelites to avoid the disaster. The head of each household was to take a lamb, slay it, eat some of it roasted, burn the rest, and put the blood on the doorposts of his house (Ex. 12:1-11). The blood was a sign that they had followed the Lord's instructions in faith (Heb. 11:28). To them God gave a promise: "When I see the blood, I will pass over you. No destructive plague will touch you when I strike Egypt" (Ex. 12:13). Furthermore, they were told that the meal was to be eaten "with your cloak tucked into your belt, your sandals on your feet and your staff in your hand" (Ex. 12:11)—that is, ready for the journey away from Egypt.

In connection with the Passover rite, the Feast of Unleavened Bread was observed. The Passover was a one-night observance whereas the Feast of Unleavened Bread lasted for seven days. Its unique feature was the exclusion of leaven from all bread. Some writers believe that the prohibition against leven was due to the belief that it was a symbol of corruption. In this case, however, it probably had more to do with the haste with which they had to leave Egypt. There was not enough time for the leaven to permeate the dough (Ex. 12:39).

These two feasts were to be observed annually throughout all generations. In this way Israelites would continually be reminded of the events on which their nation was founded. The purpose is clear: "When your children ask you, 'What does this ceremony mean to you?' then tell them, 'It is the passover sacrifice to the Lord, who passed over the houses of the Israelites in Egypt and spared our homes when he struck down the Egyptians'" (Ex. 12:26-27).

God Delivers His People

The terror of the tenth plague was enough to weaken Pharaoh's resolve. The Israelites were freed. After centuries of oppression, they marched out of Egypt toward the future. There is a strong emphasis on God's guidance and His presence in their midst. This took the form of a pillar of cloud by day and a pillar of fire by night (Ex. 13:21-22). Reference is also made to the "angel of the Lord" (Ex. 14:19-20). This phrase refers to a theophany (an appearance of God, compare Ex. 3:2) and is another way of emphasizing the guiding presence of God.

True to his nature, however, Pharaoh changed his mind. His pursuit to recapture the people led to their first crisis. "They were terrified and cried out to the Lord" (Ex. 14:10). In the face of their panic, Moses' words were all the more significant: "Do not be afraid. Stand firm and you will see the deliverance the Lord will bring you today. The Egyptians you see today you will never see again. The Lord will fight for you; you need only to be still" (vv. 13-14).

Then it happened—one of the truly dramatic moments in history! A strong east wind arose and made a path for the Israelites to march through on dry ground. The Egyptians pursued them through the same path.

Then the Lord said to Moses, "Stretch out your hand over the sea so that the waters may flow back over the Egyptians and their chariots and horsemen." Moses stretched out his hand over the sea, and at daybreak the sea went back to its place. The Egyptians were fleeing toward it, and the Lord swept them into the sea. The water flowed back and covered the chariots and horsemen—the entire army of Pharaoh that had followed the Israelites into the sea. Not one of them survived. But the Israelites went through the sea on dry ground, with a wall of water on their right and on their left. That day *the Lord saved Israel* from the hands of the Egyptians. . . . And when the Israelites saw the great power the Lord displayed against the Egyptians, the people feared the Lord and put their trust in him and Moses his servant (Ex. 14:26-30, author's italics).

Among the many lessons Israel learned from this rescue, two are of special importance. First, Israel began to learn the meaning of salvation. The verb "to save" occurs for the first time in Exodus 14:30. The meaning of the Hebrew term is "to be wide/spacious" or "to develop without hindrance." The basic meaning is freedom or victory. In this context it refers to God's victory over Pharaoh and the freedom Israel gained through deliverance from Egypt. It is used in a side variety of contexts in the Old Testament to denote victory over enemies and rescue from any dangerous situation. The deepest level of meaning, however, is found in those contexts where the emphasis is on salvation from sin (for example, Pss. 6:4; 86:1-5; Isa. 45:21-23; 61:10).[5]

Second, Israel learned that salvation is the work of God. He alone has the power to save. Throughout the Old Testament, God is the One who intervened in history to overcome His foes and save His people. He is the "Hope of Israel, its Savior in times of distress" (Jer. 14:8). Furthermore, "I, even I am the Lord, and apart from me there is no savior" (Isa. 43:11). To know God truly is to know Him as the Savior. "You know no God but me, and besides me there is no savior" (Hos. 13:4, RSV).

Beyond Israel's release from Egypt, the Exodus has an even greater significance. It points beyond itself to the continuation of God's saving activity in history. In this way, it provides a basis for hope that God would one day complete what He had begun. As one writer stated: "It is a 'sign' of the salvation to come—and the word 'sign' in this connection means an event that already contains within itself something of the reality to which it is pointing."[6] In the fullness of time, there was a "new Exodus," and it was accomplished by One greater than Moses (Heb. 3:3).

God Establishes a Covenant

The covenant established with Israel was a further fulfillment of the promise made to Abraham. Three features are basic in this new relationship. The covenant was grounded in redemption: "You your-selves have seen what I did to Egypt, and how I carried you on eagle's wings and brought you to myself" (Ex. 19:4). It was accompanied by a challenge and a promise: "Now if you obey me fully and keep my covenant, then out of all the nations you will be my treasured posses-sion" (Ex. 19:5). Finally, it involved a purpose: "Although the whole earth is mine, you will be for me a kingdom of priests and a holy nation" (Ex. 19:5-6).

This unique relation with Israel was the result of God's love and faithfulness. God was not indebted to her because of prior merit.

> The Lord did not set his affection on you and choose you because you were more numerous than other peoples. . . . It was because the Lord loved you and kept the oath he swore to your forefathers that he brought you out with a mighty hand and redeemed you from the land of slavery, from the power of Pharaoh king of Egypt. Know therefore that the Lord your God is God; he is the faithful God, keeping his covenant of love to a thousand generations of those who love him and keep his commands (Deut. 7:7-9).

Like Abraham, Israel was chosen for service. Her election was not just to privilege. It was a responsibility that would involve hardship and suffering. Israel was called to be "a holy nation" (that is, to belong exclusively to God and to be set apart for His service). As a holy nation Israel was to be "a kingdom of priests" whose vocation would be to the nations of the world.

A priest's function is to represent God to the world and the world to God. What a priest was within Israel, Israel was to be among the nations. She was a missionary priest commissioned to bring the knowledge of God to the world. "I will keep you and will make you to be a covenant for the people and a light for the Gentiles" (Isa. 42:6). In this way, Israel would fulfill the promise to Abraham that in his seed the nations of the earth would be blessed.

Israel's Failure and God's Faithfulness

Israel's Failure

Eventually Israel entered the Promised Land under Joshua, Moses' successor. The way was opened for developing a meaningful national existence. The people could live out the implications of their divine calling. Unfortunately, however, this promise was never fully realized. From the beginning, the people complained about the hardships of their new existence. Too, Canaan offered a strong temptation to compromise their faith by worshiping other gods. Israel was only too ready to yield.

The language used by the biblical writers reflect the nature of the nation's struggle. Israel is accused of committing adultery (Jer. 3:1,8; Ezek. 23:37; Hos. 7:4) and playing the harlot (Isa. 1:21; Ezek. 16:35; Hos. 3:3). This vivid language portrays the depths of Israel's unfaithfulness. It also describes accurately the religious practices of Canaan.

There were periods of economic growth. During the reigns of David and Solomon, Israel became a strong nation. After Solomon's death, the kingdom divided into the two smaller states of Israel and Judah. Both nations had difficulty maintaining their covenant loyalty and neither lived up to their high calling. Of many a ruler it had to be admitted that "he did evil in the eyes of the Lord" (1 Kings 11:6; 15:26; 16:25; 2 Kings 3:2; 8:18).

For two hundred years the two nations existed side by side. Numerous prophets labored to bring the people back to commitment to God. The prophets' messages are laced with reminders of God's goodness, calls to repentance, and warnings of God's judgment. For the most part their words fell on deaf ears. In 721 BC, the Northern Kingdom of Israel was brought to a violent end by the Assyrians. The Southern Kingdom of Judah survived until 587 BC. At that time, the Babylonians captured Jerusalem and carried its inhabitants into exile.

After the Exile, Nehemiah reflected on the fortunes of the Chosen People. His words aptly interpret their history:

> In all that has happened to us, you have been just; you have acted faithfully, while we did wrong. Our kings, our leaders, our priests and our fathers did not follow your law; they did not pay attention to your commands or the warnings you gave them. Even while they were in their kingdom, enjoying your great goodness to them in the spacious and fertile land you gave them, they did not serve you or turn from their evil ways. But see, we are slaves today, slaves in the land you gave

our forefathers so they could eat its fruit and the other good things it
produces. Because of our sins, its abundant harvest goes to the kings
you have placed over us. They rule over our bodies and our cattle as
they please. We are in great distress (Neh. 9:33-37).

Shades of Egyptian bondage! The story could be written with the
title, "From Slavery unto Slavery." The situation is similar to that
described in Genesis 11. Man's rebellion against God leads to confusion and captivity. The people chosen to be a light to the Gentiles had
walked in darkness. The nation of priests needed a sacrifice for their
own sins.

God's Faithfulness

Failure is not the last word in the Old Testament. God works
through the obedience of His people; He also works in spite of their
disobedience. For this reason, the Old Testament has a strong emphasis on hope. This hope does not rest on any power inherent in the
process of nature or history. It is grounded in the conviction that God
is faithful to His promise and that He will fulfill His purpose in history.

Israel's hope for the future was expressed in numerous images.
Some of these images include a new creation, a new kingdom, a new
age, a new covenant, an ideal ruler (Messiah), a Suffering Servant, a
Son of man, a universal outpouring of the divine Spirit. It is not possible to explore all these images here.[7] A brief survey of four representative images, however, will help us to grasp the nature of this hope
more clearly.

A new creation.—"Behold I create new heavens and a new earth.
The former things will not be remembered, nor will they come to
mind" (Isa. 65:17; compare 66:12). Salvation embraces the whole
creation. This is the most comprehensive image of hope in the Old
Testament.

The biblical view of salvation always includes the earth. The earth
was created to reflect God's glory and to provide the context for
man's obedience to God. When man rebelled against God the natural
order was also affected (Gen. 3:14-19; Rom. 8:20-21). It is not surprising, then, to find the created order itself included in the hope of

redemption. In the biblical perspective, a relationship exists between nature and the moral life of man; therefore, the earth will also share in God's final act of restoration. The individual, society, and all of nature will be purged of the effects of evil. God's glory will be manifested in all His creation.

A new covenant.—A vital part of the future was a new covenant. This aspect of Israel's hope is described in Jeremiah 31:31-34. Five characteristics of this covenant are described.

First, it would be established by God's initiative. In this passage, the pronoun "I" (referring to God) is used with five different verbs. "I will make . . . I will put . . . I will be . . . I will forgive . . . [I] will remember." Wherever relationship with God is established, God takes the first steps.

Second, the new covenant would be inward. It will not be an external law written on tablets of stone (Ex. 31:18; 34:28-29). Rather, "I will put my law within them and I will write it upon their hearts" (Jer. 31:33, RSV). The heart is the center of personality; it refers to the capacity for willing and reasoning. Unlike the old covenant, the new one would be effective because it would transform man from within (compare Jer. 24:7).

Third, it would focus on the individual. Relationship in this covenant would not be determined by family or nation. Rather, each person would come to know God through individual decision. This emphasizes the need for a personal response to God's initiative.

A fourth characteristic would be universality. " 'They will all know me, from the least of them to the greatest,' declares the Lord" (v. 34).

Finally, the new covenant would be based on forgiveness. "For I will forgive their wickedness and remember their sins no more" (v. 34). The old covenant was based on God's deliverance of Israel from physical bondage in Egypt. The new covenant would be based on God's deliverance of people from the bondage of sin. How this deliverance would be achieved Jeremiah did not say. But that God would accomplish it was certain.

The Messiah.—Another aspect of Israel's hope was the expectation of an ideal ruler from the line of David. This was based on the promise that God would establish the throne of David forever (2 Sam. 7:14). This anointed ruler ("messiah" means "anointed one") would be God's agent to restore the glory of Israel, reunite the divided kingdom and rule the nations in righteousness and peace.

The functions of the messiah-king are described in some of the most familiar passages in the Old Testament. Jeremiah proclaimed, "Behold, the days are coming, says the Lord, when I will raise up for David a righteous Branch, and he shall reign as king and deal wisely, and shall execute justice and righteousness in the land" (Jer. 23:5, RSV). Amos promised, "In that day I will . . . restore its ruins, and build it as it used to be" (Amos 9:11). Likewise, Ezekiel saw a time when "My servant David will be king over them, and they will have one shepherd. . . . and David my servant will be their prince forever" (Ezek. 37:24-25). Anyone who has heard Handel's oratorio, the *Messiah,* should recognize these words from Isaiah 9:6-7.

> For to us a child is born,
>   to us a son is given,
>   and the government will be on his
>   shoulders.
> And he will be called
>   Wonderful Counselor, Mighty God,
>   Everlasting Father, Prince of Peace.
> Of the increase of his government and
>   peace
>   there will be no end.
> He will reign on David's throne
>   and over his kingdom,
> establishing and upholding it
>   with justice and righteousness
>   from that time on and forever.

In one sense the messianic hope developed out of a situation of disappointment. The promises to the house of David created a dilemma. The reality portrayed in these promises was in sharp contrast to the experience of the people. For the most part, David's successors were disappointments. The direction of the kingdom was away from the ideal. How could such a discrepancy be explained? Oppressed by their enemies and disillusioned by unworthy rulers, the people looked to the future for a son of David who would fulfill the promises. By the time of Jesus, *Messiah* was the term which the average Jew used to point to that ideal ruler.

The Suffering Servant.—Still another aspect of Israel's hope is found in the Suffering Servant. This figure is portrayed in Isaiah 42, 49, 50, 52, and 53. These passages, called "The Songs of the Suffering Servant," are among the most remarkable in the Old Testament. In them is introduced the theme of vicarious suffering.

The first song identifies the servant as Israel. Chosen by God and filled with the Spirit, the Servant's mission is to bring justice to the nations and to be a light to the Gentiles (42:6). In the second song, the Servant is also identified with Israel (49:3). But there is a shift in emphasis: "Is it too small a thing for you to be my servant to restore the tribes of Jacob and bring back those of Israel I have kept" (v. 6). Here the Servant had a mission to Israel. Only a remnant would be restored. It was the Servant's task to call out this remnant. This has led some scholars to identify the prophet himself as the Servant.

In the third song, the suffering of the Servant is introduced. "I offered my back to those who beat me, my cheeks to those who pulled out my beard. I did not hide my face from mocking and spitting" (50:6). The servant's suffering was not due to his sins (v. 5). It was the result of his faithfulness to the mission with which God entrusted him.

The servant songs reach their grand climax in Isaiah 52:13 to 53:12. A close look at the personal pronouns *we, our, us, he, him, his* in Isaiah 53:4-6 indicates that here the Servant is neither Israel, the remnant, nor the prophet. The Servant does something for them which they cannot do for themselves. He suffers for them and thereby becomes the means of their salvation. There are several significant facets involved in this unique view of suffering.

First, it was vicarious. "Surely he took up *our infirmities* and carried *our sorrows.* . . . But he was pierced for *our transgressions*, he was crushed *for our iniquities*" (53:4-5). Furthermore, *"for* the transgression of my people he was stricken" (v. 8). and "he *bore the sin of many,* and made intercession *for the transgressors*" (v. 12). That the idea of substitution is involved is evident from these words: "*the punishment* that brought us peace *was upon him*" (v. 5) and "the Lord has laid *upon him the iniquity of us all*" (v. 6).

Also, His sufferings were redemptive in their effect. It is said that "the punishment that *brought us peace* was upon him and *by his wounds we are healed*" (v. 5). Knowing the servant "will justify many" (v. 11).

Too, the Servant's suffering was in accordance with the will of God. "The Lord has laid upon him the iniquity of us all" (v. 6). "*It was the Lord's will* to crush him and cause him to suffer . . . *the Lord makes* his life a guilt offering . . . *the will of the Lord* will prosper in his hand" (v. 10, author's italics). To say that his suffering is God's will means that it is part of the divine plan to conquer sin.

Finally, beyond suffering the Servant experienced victory. "He shall see the travail of his soul, and shall be satisfied" (v. 11, KJV) and he will receive "a portion among the great, and he will divide the spoils with the strong" (v. 12). Whether this passage implies resurrection is not clear. But it is remarkable in that it portrays the Servant's ministry coming to a climax beyond the grave.

An important question concerns the relationship of the Suffering Servant to the Messiah. Do the two images refer to the same person? The Old Testament does not make this identification explicit. Not until the New Testament is that relationship made clear. In His own person and work, Jesus fulfills the roles of Messiah and Suffering Servant. He is David's greater son and He fulfills His reign by the way of a cross. The many strands of Israel's hope come together in Him.

The saving acts of God in the Old Testament point beyond themselves. They do not contain their own conclusion. For this reason, the Old Testament does not stand by itself. It is an incomplete book. It ends in hope, but hope is unfulfilled. Only in light of the New Testament is the promise realized.

Notes

1. Maxwell Droke, ed., *The Christian Leader's Golden Treasury* (Indianapolis: Droke House, 1955), p. 218.

2. For a good discussion see H. H. Rowley, *The Biblical Doctrine of Election* (London: Lutterworth Press, 1950), pp. 45-68.

3. Roy L. Honeycutt, Jr. *Exodus, The Broadman Bible Commentary*, 1 rev., ed. Clifton J. Allen (Nashville: Broadman Press, 1969), p. 289.

4. Jews in later centuries were reluctant to pronounce the name YHWH for fear of taking it in vain. They substituted for it the word *Adonai* which means "Lord." When the Old Testament was translated into Greek, YHWH was translated by *kurios* which also means "Lord." Some translations combine the consonants of YHWH with the vowels of *Adonai*. The result is the word *Jehovah*. Many modern scholars believe that the original name was Yahweh.

5. For a summary of words used for salvation in the Old Testament see Robert L. Cate, *Old Testament Roots for New Testament Faith* (Nashville: Broadman Press, 1982), pp. 174-189.

6. Suzanne de Dietrich, *God's Unfolding Plan*, trans. Robert McAfee Brown (Philadelphia: The Westminster Press, 1976), p. 71.

7. For a survey of the different facets of Israel's hope see Anthony A. Hoekema, *The Bible and the Future* (Grand Rapids: William B. Eerdmans Publishing Co., 1979), pp. 3-12. See Stephen Travis, *I Believe in the Second Coming of Jesus* (Grand Rapids: William B. Eerdmans Publishing Co., 1982), pp. 11-48.

Bibliography

Achtemeier, Paul J. and Elizabeth. *The Old Testament Roots of Our Faith*. Philadelphia: Fortress Press, 1979.

Cole, R. Alan. *Exodus. Tyndale Old Testament Commentaries*. Edited by D. J. Wiseman. Downer's Grove, Illinois: Inter-Varsity Press, 1974.

Huey, F. B., Jr. *Exodus: A Study Guide Commentary*. Grand Rapids: Zondervan Publishing House, 1977.

Kelley, Page H. *Exodus: Called for Redemptive Mission*. Nashville: Convention Press, 1977.

LaSor, William Sanford. *Israel, a Biblical View*. Grand Rapids: William B. Eerdmans Publishing Co., 1976.

Ramm, Bernard L. *His Way Out, a Fresh Look at Exodus*. Glendale, California: G/L Publications, 1974.

Ward, Wayne E. *The Drama of Redemption*. Nashville: Broadman Press, 1966.
Wright, G. Ernest and Fuller, Reginald H. *The Book of the Acts of God*. Christian Faith Series. Edited by Reinhold Niebuhr. Garden City, N.Y.: Doubleday and Co., 1957.

3

Divine Provision: The Incarnation

The meaning of hope and fulfillment is expressed in the words of a well-known Christmas hymn.

> Come thou long-expected Jesus,
> Born to set thy people free;
> From our fears and sins release us;
> Let us find our rest in thee.
> Israel's strength and consolation,
> Hope of all the earth thou art;
> Dear desire of ev'ry nation,
> Joy of ev'ry longing heart.
> Born thy people to deliver,
> Born a child and yet a King,
> Born to reign in us forever,
> Now thy gracious kingdom bring.
> By thy own eternal spirit,
> Rule in our hearts alone;
> By thine all sufficient merit,
> Raise us to thy glorious throne.[1]

The Old Testament ends on a note of expectancy. It looks forward to the time when God would fulfill His promise. The New Testament announces the reality of the divine fulfillment. Old Testament hope is realized in Christ.

How did this take place? Paul explained: "But when the time had fully come, God sent his Son, born of a woman, born under the law, to redeem those under the law, that we might receive the full rights of sons" (Gal. 4:4-5). At the time of God's choosing, He "sent his Son." Christ's coming was not that of a prophet sent by God. He came *from*

God. Paul had in mind the whole drama of Christ's preexistence, birth, life, death, and resurrection. He thought of the Son's coming as the pivotal event in history.

The purpose of Christ's coming was "to redeem" in order that we might enjoy the rights of God's children. This means the forgiveness of sins and restoration of a right relationship to God.

That Christ came to save us from sin is the central theme of the New Testament. Joseph was instructed by the angel, "You are to give him the name Jesus, because he will save his people from their sins" (Matt. 1:21). Simeon, holding the infant Jesus in his arms, declared that He would "give his people knowledge of salvation through the forgiveness of their sins" (Luke 1:77). In seeking to restore lost people, Jesus' embodies God's own love and concern for people. This is the meaning of the stories of the lost sheep, the lost coin, and the lost son (Luke 15). Jesus summed up the meaning of His ministry, saying, "For the Son of Man came to seek and to save what was lost" (Luke 19:10).

The preaching of the apostles proclaimed the same message. The coming of Christ means that "anyone who calls on the name of the Lord will be saved" (Acts 2:21). This salvation is described as the forgiveness of sins and receiving the Holy Spirit (Acts 2:38). Furthermore, through Christ alone salvation is experienced. "Salvation is found in no other name under heaven given to men by which we must be saved" (Acts 4:12). On one occasion Paul and Barnabas were asked, "What must I do to be saved?" They responded, "Believe in the Lord Jesus Christ, and you will be saved" (Acts 16:30-31). The issue is summed up by Paul, "Christ Jesus came into the world to save sinners" (1 Tim. 1:15).

In addition, there are numerous places where Jesus was called "Savior." To shepherds the angels announced, "Today in the town of David a Savior has been born to you; he is Christ the Lord" (Luke 2:11). Samaritans confessed, "We know that this man really is the Savior of the world" (John 4:42). Peter described Him as "Prince and Savior" (Acts 5:31). Paul referred to "God our Savior" and to "Jesus Christ our Savior" in the same passage (Titus 3:4-6). John testified "that the Father has sent his Son to be the Savior of the world"

(1 John 4:14). Four times in 2 Peter, Jesus is called "Savior" (1:1,11; 3:2,18).

How are we to understand this? What is involved in the confession that Jesus is the Savior? In response to these questions, three things must be kept in mind. First, there is the unity of the Father and Son in the work of redemption. The Father should never be played over against the Son. Jesus did not accomplish our salvation *in spite* of the Father, *but because of* the Father. Paul wrote, "God was reconciling the world to himself in Christ" (2 Cor. 5:19). There is no work of God for salvation that does not finally involve Christ.[2]

Second, the life, death, and resurrection should be seen together. The death of Christ was the climax of His obedient life. His death was followed by the resurrection. Apart from the resurrection, His life and death would have been futile. Though distinct, these three aspects are inseparable in the work of salvation.

Third, the person and work of Christ cannot be separated. They may be distinguished for discussion. But in reality, they go together. Christ's work of salvation is effective because of who He is. Christ as Savior is not one of the prophets, not even the greatest of them. He is the divine Son of God.

This chapter focuses on Jesus' incarnate life. The guide for the discussion is John 1:14, "The Word became flesh and lived for a while among us."

The Word Became Flesh

The Meaning of the Incarnation

The word *incarnation* comes from a Latin term meaning "en-flesh-ment." Though the word is not found in the Bible, it proclaims a biblical truth—the truth expressed in John 1:14, "The Word became flesh and lived for a while among us." In biblical faith, therefore, the incarnation means that the preexistent Son of God became a man. At a particular time and place, He entered the world in a unique way and was subject to the limitations of human existence.

The Biblical Witness to the Incarnation

The New Testament was written from the perspective of belief in the incarnate Christ. Listening to some of its witnesses will help us understand more clearly what is involved in this belief.

The Witness of Paul.—Paul spoke of God "sending His own Son in the likeness of sinful man" (Rom. 8:3). "Likeness" does not imply that the Son's humanity is unreal. It means that He came to dwell in the same human nature where sin came to dwell. He invaded the territory occupied by sin, but He did it without becoming sinful.

Again, Paul stated, "For you know the grace of our Lord Jesus Christ, that he was rich, yet for your sakes he became poor" (2 Cor. 8:9). The contrast between "rich" and "poor" is the difference between Christ's preexistent glory and the condescension involved in becoming human. The motivation for this movement from heaven to earth was "the grace of our Lord Jesus Christ."

What this means is explained more fully in the following words:

Have this mind among yourselves, which is yours in Christ Jesus, who, though he was in the form of God, did not count equality with God a thing to be grasped, but emptied himself, taking the form of a servant, being born in the likeness of men. And being found in human form he humbled himself and became obedient unto death, even death on a cross (Phil. 2:5-8, RSV).

This passage expresses several truths. (1) Christ was preexistent with God. (2) He became a man, the incarnation. (3) His incarnation was voluntary. (4) His life on earth was lived as an obedient servant. (5) His obedience led to His death on a cross. The last two ideas are echoes of the Suffering Servant of Isaiah 53.

The witness of Hebrews.—This epistle begins by affirming the deity and preexistence of Christ. He is the fulfillment of the word God spoke through the prophets (1:1). He is also the "heir of all things" and the agent through whom God created the universe (v. 2). Furthermore, "The Son is the radiance of God's glory and the exact representation of his being, sustaining all things by his powerful word" (v. 3).

Against this transcendent background, the writer spoke of the incarnation. Christ "was made a little lower than the angels" (2:9). Because the people He came to save "have flesh and blood, he too shared their humanity" (v. 14). To accomplish His purpose, "He had to be made like his brothers in every way" (v. 17).

The witness of John.—The most detailed discussion of the incarnation is in the prologue to John's Gospel (1:1-18). By beginning his story of Jesus with the incarnation, John differed from the first three Gospels. They began from within history. Mark began with Jesus' baptism in the Jordan. Matthew began with the genealogy of Jesus. Luke started with the birth of John the Baptist as a prelude to Jesus' birth. The starting point for each writer was determined by his context, his audience, and his purpose. For John these factors suggested an approach from the perspective of eternity. From this vantage point, he saw Jesus as the Word of God.

Word was an important term in the ancient world. For a Greek, it meant reason and order. It stood for the principle of rationality and order in the universe. Because of the presence of *word*, the world is a cosmos rather than a chaos. In this view, however, *word* is more of a philosophical principle than a personal power.

In the Old Testament, *word* is associated with God. The word of God is God's personal power in action. Through His word, God created the world (Gen. 1; Ps. 33:6), spoke to the prophets (Jer, 1:2; Ezek. 2:1; Joel 1:1), and accomplished His purpose in history (Ps. 107:20; Isa. 55:11). This dynamic understanding of "word" shaped John's thought about Jesus.

John illumined the meaning of the incarnation by making six assertions about the Word of God.

(1) The Word is eternal. "In the beginning was the Word" (1:1). The Gospel begins with the same phrase as Genesis 1:1. Genesis describes the original creation. John wrote of the new creation. Both are attributed to the Word of God. But John went back beyond the beginning. When the world was created, the Word already was.

(2) The Word is personal. "The Word was with God. . . . He was with God in the beginning" (vv. 1-2). The phrase "with God" means "face to face with God." It expresses the very closest relationship.

The relationship is a personal one. This is made clear in John 17:5 when Jesus prayed, "Father, glorify me in your presence with the glory I had with you before the world began."

(3) The Word is divine. "The Word was God" (1:1). The Word shares in the nature and being of God. The *New English Bible* says, "What God was, the Word was." The words and deeds of Jesus are the words and deeds of God. This is the basis for the Christian belief that Jesus and God are one in nature and purpose though distinct in person and function.

(4) The Word is the agent of creation. "Through him all things were made; without him nothing was made that has been made" (v. 3; Heb. 1:2). This is an allusion to Genesis 1. It was expanded by Paul in Colossians 1:16-17. There he affirmed that Christ was before all things (v. 17), Christ created all things (v. 16), and Christ holds all things together.

(5) The Word is life and light. "In him was life and that life is the light of men" (v. 4). As the agent of creation, the Word is also the source of life-giving power. He sustains life in the universe (compare Heb. 1:3) and is the source of spiritual life which God desires to give (John 5:24-26; 10:10; 14:6). The life is also light. The Word which is the source of moral light through creation is also the redemptive light which dispels the darkness of sin (3:19; 8:12; 12:46).

(6) The Word became incarnate. "The Word became flesh and lived for a while among us" (v. 14). With this statement, the prologue reaches a climax. The eternal and creative Word of God became the man Jesus of Nazareth. The flesh He became was not a heavenly humanity of a different order. It was the same humanity as ours (apart from sin).

It is difficult to imagine a more staggering claim. Our minds cannot penetrate its depths. Given the difference between God and man, Creator and creation, the incarnation is the deepest mystery of the Christian faith.

The Purpose of the Incarnation

Incarnation and revelation.—Can we know God? What is He really like? Many thoughtful people have asked these questions. The incarnation provides the answer. "No one has seen God, but God the only Son, who is at the Father's side, has made him known" (John 1:18). If we want to know what God is like, we must look at Jesus. He is the living commentary on the character of God. He is the human face of God. He is the window through which we see the heart of God. To Philip's request, "Lord, show us the Father," Jesus responded, "Anyone who has seen me has seen the Father" (John 14:8-9).

Paul spoke of Jesus as the "image of the invisible God" (Col. 1:15). This means that He is the authentic likeness of God. This likeness is given in a human life. God is projected on the screen of history for people to see in Jesus Christ. He is "the radiance of God's glory and the exact representation of his being" (Heb. 1:3).

Of course, Jesus is not the only revelation of God. God made Himself known to His people in the Old Testament. "In the past God spoke to our forefathers through the prophets at many times and in various ways, but in these last days he has spoken to us by his Son" (Heb. 1:1-2). The revelation to the prophets was true, but it was partial and preparatory. The revelation in Christ is complete and definitive. All revelation must, therefore, be interpreted in the light of Him. Any supposed revelation of God that contradicts what we know of Him in Christ cannot be true.

This does not mean that any of us has comprehended all of God's revelation in Christ. It stretches our human capacities as far as they can go. Paul's words in 1 Corinthians 13:12 are helpful at this point: "Now I know in part." "I know" means that our knowledge is real and true. We do not have to opt for agnosticism. "In part" is a reminder of our human limitations. We do not know everything. There will always be a dimension of mystery. Thus, the apostle confessed, "No one would deny that this religion of ours is a tremendous mystery, resting as it does on the one who appeared in human flesh" (1 Tim. 3:16, Phillips).

Incarnation and the cross.—The incarnation finds its deepest meaning in the cross. "The Word became flesh" (John 1:14) must be interpreted by "Christ died for our sins" (1 Cor. 15:3).

The passages in the New Testament which begin with the incarnation point to the crucifixion. For example, Paul said that, in becoming man, Christ "humbled himself and became obedient unto death— even death on a cross!" (Phil 2:8). The condenscension which began in eternity was completed on the cross.

The writer of Hebrews stated that Christ "had to be made like his brothers in every way, in order that he might become a merciful and faithful high priest in service to God, and that he might make atonement for the sins of the people" (Heb. 2:17). Because He was one with us in our humanity, He is able to function as our High Priest. As our High Priest, He does two things: (1) He represents us before God and (2) He offers the sacrifice for our sins.

For John the eternal Word who became a man is also "the Lamb of God who takes away the sin of the world"! (John 1:29). In each of these references, the movement is from heaven to Bethlehem to Calvary.

The Means of the Incarnation

The incarnation tells us that Jesus came into the world as a man. The virgin birth tells us the way He came into the world. He came by being conceived in the womb of Mary by the power of the Holy Spirit (Matt. 1:18; Luke 1:35). At the time of her conception, Mary was engaged to Joseph (Matt. 1:18). She was still a virgin (Luke 1:34). Mary remained a virgin until Jesus was born (Matt. 1:25). To the angelic announcement that she would conceive and bear a son, Mary responded, "How will this be . . . since I am a virgin? The angel answered, 'The Holy Spirit will come upon you, and the power of the Most High will overshadow you'" (Luke 1:34-35). This does not mean that the Holy Spirit is the "father" of Jesus. It means that according to His human nature Jesus had no father at all. His miraculous conception took place solely by the will and word of God. In this way, it is similar to the creation of the world at the beginning. From the earliest times, the truth of this story has been part of the church's confession.[3]

Objections to the virgin birth.—Nevertheless, many objections to the virgin birth have been raised.

One objection comes from science. It is that such a conception is biologically impossible. The laws of nature do not allow for an event of this kind. In response, it must be admitted that the virgin birth cannot be explained scientifically. It is a miracle. Apart from the power of God, there is no explanation. As a miracle, it is part of the larger mystery of the incarnation and must be accepted by faith. Whether one believes or denies the virgin birth will depend on one's view of God and His relation to the world He created.

Another objection comes from mythology. In this view, the virgin birth is compared to Roman and Greek myths. In these mythical tales, the gods produced children by having sexual relations with their female cohorts. The Greek god Zeus, for example, is said to have fathered Hercules, Perseus, and Alexander. A comparison of these stories with the New Testament reveals profound differences. The birth narratives in Matthew and Luke are marked by an ethical sensitivity not found in the ancient myths. The New Testament emphasizes God's ability to accomplish His purpose in history. It has nothing to do with divine-human cohabitation.

Still another objection comes from theology. Can one who is miraculously conceived really be one with us? The response to this question is twofold. (1) The miraculous conception does not argue against Jesus' humanity. The fact that Jesus was formed in the womb of Mary, was born, lived, and died is sufficient to establish His oneness with us. (2) It is not sin that makes us human. Sin dehumanizes us. Jesus came to restore humanity to its original purpose. His humanity was perfect. It was what God intended when He created Adam. If we want to see true humanity, we must look at the last Adam rather than the first.

A final objection is based on the "silence" of the New Testament. It is pointed out that the virgin birth is recorded by only Matthew and Luke. There is no explicit mention of it anywhere else in the New Testament. This objection involves the issue of biblical authority. How many writers have to mention an event before it can be believed? The birth stories are undeniably part of the earliest manuscripts of Matthew and Luke. This is sufficient to make them a valid part of the New Testament witness to Christ.

The meaning of the virgin birth.—What, then, is the meaning of the virgin birth? What light does it shed on God's saving activity in history?

The virgin birth is the first stage in the fulfillment of God's saving purpose. It heralds the dawn of the messianic age. The genealogies of Matthew and Luke provide a clue on this point.

Matthew was especially interested in fulfillment. Writing for a Jewish audience, Matthew wanted to show that the Old Testament points to Christ. His Gospel opens with the genealogy of Jesus. "A record of the genealogy of Jesus Christ the Son of David, the Son of Abraham" (Matt. 1:1). Mention of David and Abraham is a reminder that Jesus' birth was not an isolated event. It brought to a climax the salvation history that began with Abraham. Jesus is both the seed of Abraham and the ideal ruler from David's line.

Luke was also interested in fulfillment. But his perspective was broader than Matthew's. Writing for Gentiles, Luke was interested in showing the continuity of Jesus with all mankind. Luke's genealogy of Jesus goes back beyond Abraham. He identified Jesus as "the Son of Adam, the Son of God" (Luke 3:38). In this way, Luke emphasized that Jesus' mission was not only for Israel but for humanity as a whole. Thus, Jesus is the second Adam, the head of a new race and the beginning of a new humanity (compare Rom. 5:12-21).

Furthermore, the virgin birth is a witness to the humanity and deity of Christ. That He was born is evidence of His humanity. But His birth does not explain all that He is. The Word that became flesh did not originate in Bethlehem. At Bethlehem, the Word entered uniquely into the world for our salvation. But behind this event is eternity. Christ came from God. This observation does not prove the deity of Christ. But it is consistent with such a claim.

The earliest followers of Jesus did not believe in Jesus' deity because they first believed in His miraculous birth. First they experienced all He had done for them in His life, death, and resurrection. Jesus had done for them what only God could do. After the resurrection and under the leading of the Holy Spirit, they acknowledged Jesus as Lord and Son of God. They understood that He really was "Immanuel . . . God with us" (Matt. 1:23). In the light of this confession, the story of His birth was believed and preserved.

Finally, the virgin birth reminds us that salvation is a divine gift not a human achievement. Man cannot save himself. He could not even introduce the Savior into human society. Our salvation is wholly dependent on God's grace. The Savior came into the world through a miraculous birth from above. He is God's gift, just as the salvation He effected is God's gift of grace.

And Lived Among Us for a While

The Gospels do not move immediately from Jesus' birth to His death. There is an emphasis on the life He lived and the ministry He performed. The records we have in the New Testament do not tell us all about the life of Jesus. They focus on His public ministry and the events leading up to the crucifixion. Apart from the birth stories in Matthew and Luke, only one incident of Jesus' early life is recorded (Luke 2:41-52).

It is not wrong, therefore, to see Jesus' life as a prelude to the cross. But it would be wrong to pass over it as if it were of minor significance only. His life, as well as His death and resurrection, was part of God's saving activity. Its significance can be described in several ways.

Jesus' Life Grounds Christian Faith in History

The Christian belief that God entered history in the person of Christ is distinctive. No other religion makes such a claim for its founder. Christians also believe in the risen Lord whom they confess is the same Jesus of Nazareth who lived and died almost two thousand years ago. To use modern terms, the Jesus of history and the Christ of faith are one and the same.

Christian faith, therefore, does not rest on speculative ideas. It is rooted in a real person who lived at a particular time and place. Ideas are certainly a part of Christian faith. Doctrine is essential to the integrity of faith and life. But these doctrines cannot be detached from the life of Jesus. If they are separated from Him, they lose their real meaning. As one writer stated, "Jesus was born of a virgin, lived, died, rose from the dead. Those were not general truths of philosophy; they were facts of history."[4] It should be added that these are facts interpreted by faith. But the point is valid. Thus, knowledge of the historical Jesus is necessary and historical research into the New Testament should be encouraged.

Jesus' Life Establishes His Identity with Us

The life of Jesus confirms the reality of His incarnation. It also shows that His human experiences were genuine. There was no make-believe on His part. He truly experienced human life. He knows us not only because of His role in creation. He knows us from experience. He is no stranger to human life.

We come into the world through the process of birth; so did He. "When the time had fully come, God sent his Son, born of a woman, born under law" (Gal. 4:4). We grow physically, mentally, and spiritually; so did He. "And Jesus grew in wisdom and stature, and in favor with God and men" (Luke 2:52). We experience temptation; so did He. Jesus "has been tempted in every way, just as we are—yet was without sin" (Heb. 4:15; compare Matt. 4:1-11; Luke 4:1-13). We experience hunger; so did He. "He ate nothing during those days, and at the end of them he was hungry" (Luke 4:2). We become physically weary; He did too. "Jesus, tired as he was from the journey, sat down by the well" (John 4:6). We often experience rejection; He experienced this also. "From this time many of his disciples turned back and no longer followed him" (John 6:66; compare 1:11). We experience physical pain; He was no stranger to this either. "Then Pilate took Jesus and had him flogged. The soldiers twisted together a crown of thorns and put it on his head" (John 19:1-2). We undergo anguish and stress; so did He. "And being in anguish, he prayed more earnestly, and his sweat was like drops of blood falling to the ground" (Luke 22:44). We die; this experience, too, was His. "Jesus called out with a loud voice, 'Father, into your hands I commit my spirit.' When he had said this, he breathed his last" (Luke 23:46). In all of these experiences and more, He was one with us.

This fact provides a source of genuine encouragement. No one can rightly say, "God does not care!" or "God can't possibly understand what I'm going through!" He does care. He cared so much that in Christ He became involved in human life. He also understands. A great Puritan preacher once said, "Christ leads through no darker door than he's been through before."[5]

Jesus' identification with us in this way has not always been accepted. Late in the first century, some people denied His humanity. They were called "Docetists." This term is from a Greek word which means "to seem" or "to appear." They believed that Jesus only seemed to be human. He was a real man only in appearance. This view was based on the idea that the material world is inherently evil. Thus, God cannot come into contact with matter. Such a view has serious implications for the Christian faith. It undermines the biblical view of creation as God's *good* work (compare Gen. 1:31). It also denies the biblical view of salvation. If the Docetists were right, the Word could not become flesh. John resisted this in the strongest possible terms. "This is how you can recognize the Spirit of God: Every spirit that acknowledges that Jesus Christ has come in the flesh is from God, but every spirit that does not acknowledge Jesus is not from God" (1 John 4:2-3; compare 2 John 7).

Jesus' Life Embodies the Reality of the Kingdom of God

The dominant theme in Jesus' ministry was the kingdom of God. In the Gospels, the phrase itself is used over one hundred times. Numerous references to the kingdom occur where the exact phrase is absent. We should note here Matthew's preference for "kingdom of heaven." The change may have been due to reverence for the divine name. If the wording is different, the meaning is the same.

Jesus began His public ministry proclaiming, "The time has come. . . . The kingdom of God is near. Repent and believe the good news!" (Mark 1:14). He ended his earthly ministry speaking to His disciples "about the kingdom of God" (Acts 1:3).

The meaning of the kingdom.—Usually when we think of a kingdom we think of a territory or realm over which a king rules. This meaning may be present in the New Testament, but it is secondary. The primary meaning is God's rule or reign. It is a dynamic concept. The emphasis is on God exercising His royal rule.[6]

In the first century AD, several ideas were associated with the concept of kingdom. A major one involved hope for the restoration of

David's kingdom through a ruler from that royal line. Thoughts of commitment to God, faithfulness to the law, and forgiveness of sins were not excluded. But centuries of foreign domination and oppression had intensified the political nature of that hope. By the time of Jesus, many Jews looked for a warrior king who would defy the might of Rome and restore the glory of Israel.

The kingdom as present.—In Christ the kingdom was a dynamic, present reality. This is evident from Christ's words. When Pharisees asked Him when the kingdom would come, Jesus responded, "Behold, the kingdom of God is in the midst of you" (Luke 17:20, RSV). When critics quizzed Him about casting out demons, He answered, "But if I drive out demons by the Spirit of God, then the kingdom has come upon you" (Matt. 12:28; compare Luke 11:20). When disciples asked Him about parables, He explained, "The secret of the kingdom has been given to you" (Mark 4:11). On another occasion, He said to His disciples, "Blessed are the eyes that see what you see. For I tell you that many prophets and kings wanted to see what you see but did not see it, and to hear what you hear but did not hear it" (Luke 10:23-24). Earlier generations lived in unfulfilled expectations. Jesus' followers were experiencing the actual inbreaking of the kingdom.

The presence of the kingdom is also evident in the miracles Jesus performed. These mighty works are an indispensable part of Jesus' ministry. They occur in all of the Gospels. Almost one third of Mark's Gospel is devoted to them. An early Christian preacher recalled "how God anointed Jesus of Nazareth with the Holy Spirit and power, and how he went around doing good and healing all who were under the power of the devil, because God was with him" (Acts 10:38).

The miracles usually fall into four basic categories. First, there are miracles of healing. Examples are the paralytic (Mark 2:1-12) and the lame man by the pool of Bethesda (John 5:1-8). Second, there is exorcism or casting out demons. Examples are the Gerasene demoniac (Mark 5:1-19) and the boy with an evil spirit (Mark 9:14-27). Third, there is raising the dead. Two examples are Lazarus (John 11:11-44) and the son of the widow of Nain (Luke 7:11-17). A final category concerns Jesus' power over nature. Well-known instances include the calming of the storm (Mark 4:35-41) and walking on water (Mark 6:45-52).

There was nothing of the exhibitionism about Jesus which characterized many of the magicians of that day. He did not perform miracles to seduce people into following Him. He refused to dazzle people by casting Himself from the pinnacle of the Temple (Matt. 4:5-7). He also refused to perform signs to satisfy the curiosity of the crowds (Luke 11:29). Jesus was no Simon Magus, interested in power for personal gain.

A clue to the significance of the miracles is found in the words used to describe them. One word is *dunamis*. It means "power" or "mighty work." Our word *dynamite* comes from it. The New Testament depicts God as the source of all power. "For nothing is impossible with God" (Luke 1:37). Jesus is the embodiment of God's power (1 Cor. 1:24). The mighty works of Jesus reveal the power of God in action. A second word is *teras* which means "wonder." This word describes the reaction of those who receive or observe the effects of a miracle. It is used in the New Testament only in connection with the third word, *sēmeia*. *Sēmeia* means "sign." A sign is something that points beyond itself to another reality.

In the New Testament, therefore, the miracles are not thought of as violations of the natural order. They are signals of the new order. They pointed to the inbreaking of God's reign in Christ. They indicated that the messianic age had dawned. On one occasion John the Baptist sent his disciples to ask Jesus, "Are you the one who was to come, or should we expect someone else?" Jesus replied, "Go back and report to John what you hear and see: The blind receive sight, the lame walk, those who have leprosy are cured, the deaf hear, the dead are raised, and the good news is preached to the poor" (Matt. 11:2-5). The language of Jesus' response comes from Isaiah 61:1, indicating that in His miracles the messianic predictions were being fulfilled.

The mighty works are also indications of what will happen when the kingdom of God comes in all of its fulness. They are windows through which we catch a glimpse of the way things are in God's kind of world. As such, they are promises which inspire hope. They point us to the completion of God's saving activity in the future. Then there will be no more sorrow or tears. Death, the last enemy, will be finally overcome.[7]

The kingdom as future.—God's reign is present in Christ. But there is also a future dimension to the kingdom. For example, the kingdom is often associated with the final judgment.

> Not everyone who says to me, "Lord, Lord," will enter *the kingdom of heaven,* but only he who does the will of my Father who is in heaven. Many will say to me *on that day,* "Lord, Lord, did we not prophesy in your name, and in your namè drive out demons and perform many miracles?" Then I will tell them plainly, "I never knew you. Away from me, you evil doers!" (Matt. 7:21-23, author's italics; compare Luke 13:22-30; Matt. 25:31-46).

At the Last Supper, Jesus spoke of the kingdom as future. "I tell you the truth, I will not drink again of the fruit of the vine *until that day* when I drink it *anew in the kingdom of God*" (Mark 14:25, author's italics; compare Matt. 26:29; Luke 22:18).

Because of the life and ministry of Christ, we can experience the reality of the kingdom now. But present experience is only a foretaste of the fullness which is to come. One scholar has compared the present and future dimensions of the kingdom to D day and V-day.[8] Looking back on World War II, we know that D day was the turning point of the war in Europe. The invasion was decisive for the final victory. Victory did not come immediately; but in time, it did come. The incarnation of Jesus, His life, death, and resurrection is God's D day. The decisive battle has been fought. The tide of battle against sin has been turned. But V-day is still future. In the meantime, we wait in hope.

The kingdom and the King.—Jesus fulfilled the Old Testament hope for a messianic king. But He did not fulfill the expectation of His contemporaries for a warrior king. He came rather as the Suffering Servant of Isaiah 53. People expected Him to embrace the throne by destroying the Romans. But He ascended the throne by embracing the cross.

The nature of Jesus' kingship was announced at His baptism. At the beginning of His public ministry, Jesus was baptized by John the Baptist. John had come "preaching a baptism of repentance for the forgiveness of sins" (Mark 1:4). As sinless, Jesus did not need to repent and receive forgiveness. For Jesus, baptism was His public dedication to do the will of God. When John showed reluctance to baptize Jesus, Jesus responded, "Let it be so now; it is proper for us to do this to fulfill all righteousness" (Matt. 3:15). Jesus approved John's baptizing as a work of God. Too, there may be significance in this symbolic association of Himself with sinners whom He came to save (Isa. 53:12).

When Jesus came up from the water, the heavens opened and God said, "This is my Son, whom I love; with Him I am well pleased" (Matt. 3:17). The first part of this statement ("This is my Son") comes from Psalm 2:7. Psalm 2 is addressed to God's anointed one (messiah) from the house of David. The second part of the statement ("whom I love; with him I am well pleased") comes from Isaiah 42:1. Isaiah 42 introduces the servant of Yahweh. In other words, Jesus was combining in His life and ministry two great themes from the Old Testament: the messianic king and the Suffering Servant.

In the Old Testament, an endowment of the Spirit was associated both with the Messiah and the Servant. Of the Messiah, it was said, "The Spirit of the Lord will rest on him" (Isa. 11:2). Of the Servant, God stated, "I will put my Spirit on him" (Isa. 42:1). So at His baptism, Jesus "saw the Spirit of God descending like a dove and lighting on him" (Matt. 3:16). This does not mean that Jesus did not possess the Spirit before His baptism. The Spirit is presented here as the power of God equipping Him for His ministry of service and suffering. Later, in the synagogue at Nazareth, Jesus recalled this moment. In the words of Isaiah 61:1-2, He declared, "The Spirit of the Lord is on me, because he has anointed me to preach good news to the poor. He has sent me to proclaim freedom for the prisoners and recovery of sight for the blind, to release the oppressed, to proclaim the year of the Lord's favor" (Luke 4:18-19; compare Acts 10:38).

The nature of Jesus' kingship was tested in the wilderness (Matt. 4:11; Mark 1:12-13; Luke 4:1-13). The temptation in the wilderness took place shortly after the baptism. Jesus had just committed Himself to a ministry of service and suffering. Such a view of the Messiah flew in the face of popular hopes. The temptation experience put Jesus' resolve to the test. Each test presented an alternate route to the kingdom—routes designed to bypass the cross.

The first alternate route concerned bread. "If you are the Son of God, tell these stones to become bread" (Matt. 4:3). The immediate appeal was to satisfy Jesus' own hunger. But beyond that was the appeal to be a bread-dispensing king. In a land where people often knew famine, this idea had a strong appeal. People expected the Messiah to repeat the miracles of Moses' time, especially the miracle of the manna (Ex. 16; John 6:30 *ff.*). All people want bread, but they may have no interest in hearing the Word of God. No doubt Jesus was concerned about bread (compare Matt. 14:13-21). But He was aware of needs deeper than the physical. Hence, He offered Himself as the "bread of life" (John 6:48).

The second alternate route concerned miracles. Jesus was invited to cast Himself from the highest point of the Temple and call on angels to save Him (Matt. 4:6). The immediate appeal was to play to the gallery. There was one tradition that the Messiah would appear suddenly in the Temple (Mal. 3:1-2). Jesus could gain a quick and easy following by performing such a wonder. But Jesus would not put God to the wrong kind of test by pandering to those who craved signs.

The third alternate route concerned the kingdoms of the world. The immediate appeal was to take a shortcut to glory and power. Satan sought to lure Jesus into compromise. But Jesus had come to destroy the works of the devil (1 John 1:8). Such a goal could not be achieved by compromise with the enemy. He rejected the worldly way to power.

Luke wrote, "When the devil had finished all this tempting, he left him until an opportune time" (Luke 4:13). Jesus won an initial victory. But these same temptations recurred throughout Jesus' ministry.

The nature of Jesus' kingship was questioned by a disciple (Matt. 16:13-23; Mark 8:27-33). Because of the time spent with Jesus, the disciples had already formed an opinion of Him. So Jesus' question, "Who do you say I am?" (Matt. 16:15), hardly came as a surprise.

Peter, spokesman for the group, replied, "You are the Christ, the Son of the living God" (Matt. 16:16). The answer was important. It indicated a shift in their thinking. Jesus' words and works had not measured up to their preconceived ideas. Nevertheless, they confessed Him as Messiah. But their progress was not complete.

Jesus accepted the confession. From that time on He began to teach the disciples what it meant to be the Messiah. He explained that it involved suffering and death. But this would not be the end. After His death, He would be raised to life (v. 21). Peter rebuked Jesus, "'Never, Lord!' he said, 'This shall never happen to you!'" (v. 22). In spite of the progress he had made, there was still no room in Peter's mind for a suffering Messiah. Jesus' rebuke of Peter was even more severe. "Out of my sight, Satan! You are a stumbling block to me; you do not have in mind the things of God, but the things of men" (v. 23). Peter presented to Jesus the same temptation He had faced in the wilderness. It was the temptation to take an alternate route to the kingdom—one that did not involve suffering and death.

The nature of Jesus' kingship was reaffirmed in His transfiguration (Matt. 17:1-8; Mark 9:2-8; Luke 9:28-36). With three disciples, Jesus went up into a mountain to pray. While He was praying, He underwent a striking change of appearance (Matt. 17:2). Such a change suggests a manifestation of the glory of God in Christ (John 1:14; 17:5; 2 Pet. 1:17).

In the midst of the glory, Moses and Elijah appeared. Luke said that they talked with Jesus "about his departure, which he was about to bring to fulfillment at Jerusalem" (Luke 9:31). The word "departure" is literally "exodus." The reference is to what Jesus would accomplish through His death and resurrection. Moses led the people of God in an Exodus from Egyptian bondage. Jesus is the new and greater Moses. He would lead people out of the bondage of sin.

In this experience, as at the baptism, God spoke. The words were the same. "This is my son, whom I love; with him I am well pleased" (Matt. 17:5). Once again words from Psalm 2:7 and Isaiah 42:1 played a role. For Jesus, they were confirmation of His role as Messiah and Servant of the Lord. But the message was also for the disciples. They did not fully understand the route Jesus had chosen. At any moment, one of them could become a stumbling block to Him. Peter had just shown how it could happen. Their task was not to propose alternate routes for Jesus to follow. It was to follow Him down the one route He had chosen. Hence the command, "Listen to him!" (Matt. 17:5).

Eventually, the nature of Jesus' kingship was sealed by His sacrifice and vindicated by His resurrection. Along the way, He resisted every effort to turn Him aside from the will of God. The depth of Jesus' commitment can be seen in His experience in Gethsemane. There Jesus faced the reality of His coming death. At first, He seemed to draw back from it. "Father, if you are willing, take this cup from me" (Luke 22:42). The cup represented all that was involved in His passion. Certainly, more than physical death was involved. People have often faced physical death with a song on their lips. Almost four hundred years earlier the Greek philosopher, Socrates, met death by calmly drinking hemlock.

But Jesus faced something no one had ever faced before or would ever face again. He was not a philosopher dying for a principle; nor was He a martyr dying for a noble cause. He was the sinless Son of God facing death for the sins of the world. He was about to bear the sins of the world in His own body.

To draw back momentarily from such a task is no sign of cowardice. His final words are the clue. "Yet not my will, but yours be done" (Luke 22:42). It was the final measure of surrender. It represents a reversal of the sin of the first Adam. In the garden of Eden, Adam declared in effect, "Not thy will be done, but mine." The result turned the garden into a wilderness. Christ's dedication to the Father's purpose will eventually turn the wilderness into a garden (Rev. 22:1-5).

Notes

1. Charles Wesley, "Come, Thou Long-Expected Jesus," *Baptist Hymnal* (Nashville: Convention Press, 1975), p. 79.
2. This involves the issue of God's Trinitarian nature. For helpful, brief discussions see Fisher Humphreys, *The Nature of God, Layman's Library of*

Christian Doctrine (Nashville: Broadman Press, 1985), 4, pp. 128-139 and Shirley C. Guthrie, Jr., *Christian Doctrine,* (Atlanta: John Knox Press, 1968), pp. 89-106.

3. Good discussions of the virgin birth are found in F. F. Bruce, "The Person of Christ: Incarnation, Virgin Birth," *Christianity Today* 4 (October 13, 1961), pp. 30-31 and Millard J. Erickson, *Christian Theology* 3 vols. (Grand Rapids: Baker Book House, 1983-85), 1:739-58.

4. W. T. Conner, *The Gospel of Redemption,* p. 80.

5. Quoted in Donald G. Miller, "Why God Became Man," *Interpretation* 23 (October, 1969) :424.

6. Robert H. Stein, *The Method and Message of Jesus' Teachings,* pp. 60-79.

7. Alan Richardson, *The Miracle Stories of the Gospels.*

8. Oscar Cullmann, *Christ and Time,* rev. ed., trans. Floyd V. Filson, (Philadelphia: The Westminster Press), 1964.

Bibliography

Bruce, F. F. *What the Bible Teaches About What Jesus Did. The Layman's Series.* Wheaton, Illinois: Tyndale House Publishers, Inc., 1979.

Ellis, E. Earle. *The Gospel of Luke. The New Century Bible Commentary.* Ed. by Matthew Black. Grand Rapids: William B. Eerdmans Publishing Co., 1981.

Fisher, Fred L. *Jesus and His Teachings.* Nashville: Broadman Press, 1972.

Green, Michael, ed. *The Truth of God Incarnate.* Grand Rapids: William B. Eerdmans Publishing Co., 1977.

Hendricks, William L. *Who Is Jesus Christ? Layman's Library of Christian Doctrine,* 2. Nashville: Broadman Press, 1985.

Hunter, Archibald M. *The Work and Words of Jesus.* Rev. ed. Philadelphia: The Westminster Press, 1973.

Manson, T. W. *The Servant Messiah.* Reprint ed. Cambridge: Cambridge University Press, 1966.

Neill, Stephen. *The Supremacy of Jesus.* The Jesus Library. Edited by Michael Green. Downers Grove, Illinois: Inter-Varsity Press, 1984.

Richardson, Alan. *The Miracle Stories of the Gospels.* London: SCM Press Ltd., 1959.

Stein, Robert H. *The Method and Message of Jesus' Teachings.* Philadelphia: The Westminster Press, 1978.

Stewart, James S. *The Life and Teaching of Jesus Christ.* Nashville: Abingdon Press, n.d.

Summers, Ray. *Commentary on Luke.* Waco, Texas: Word Books, Publishers, 1972.

4

Divine Provision: The Cross

Jesus' earthly ministry ended with His public execution. The New Testament tells the story simply, but graphically.

> When they came to the place called The Skull, there they crucified him, along with the criminals—one on his right, the other on his left. Jesus said "Father, forgive them, for they do not know what they are doing." And they divided up his clothes by casting lots. The people stood watching, and the rulers even sneered at him. They said, "He saved others; let him save himself if he is the Christ of God, the Chosen One." The soldiers also came up and mocked him. They offered him wine vinegar and said, "If you are the king of the Jews, save yourself." There was a written notice above him, which read: THIS IS THE KING OF THE JEWS. One of the criminals who hung there hurled insults at him: "Aren't you the Christ? Save yourself and us!" But the other criminal rebuked him. "Don't you fear God," he said, "since you are under the same sentence? We are punished justly, for we are getting what our deeds deserve. But this man has done nothing wrong." Then he said, "Jesus, remember me when you come into your kingdom." Jesus answered him, "I tell you the truth, today you will be with me in paradise." It was now about the sixth hour, and darkness came over the whole land until the ninth hour, for the sun stopped shining. And the curtain of the temple was torn in two. Jesus called out with a loud voice, "Father, into your hands I commit my spirit," When he had said this, he breathed his last (Luke 23:33-46).

The cross is the supreme symbol of the Christian faith. No other symbol can compare with it in importance. It has been the dominant theme in art and architecture, music and literature, faith and conduct. In a sense, it is a strange symbol. Crucifixion was an unusually cruel way to die. It was a form of death reserved for criminals. Yet, what was for the ancient world the mark of shame became for Christians a symbol of glory. The attitude of the earliest Christians is summed up in these words: "May I never boast except in the cross of our Lord Jesus Christ" (Gal. 6:14).

How did such a transformation take place? Through faith, Christians see in the cross the high point of God's saving activity.

> For the message of the cross is foolishness to those who are perishing, but to us who are being saved it is the power of God. . . . God was pleased through the foolishness of what was preached to save those who believe. Jews demand miraculous signs and Greeks look for wisdom, but we preach Christ crucified: a stumbling block to Jews and foolishness to Gentiles, but to those whom God has called, both Jews and Greeks, Christ the power of God and the wisdom of God (1 Cor. 1:18-24).

A scene in John Bunyan's *The Pilgrim's Progress,* illustrates the meaning of the cross. The main character, Christian, left the City of Destruction, burdened with his sin. His agonizing question was, "What shall I do to be saved?" Evangelist directed him to the wicket-gate. Having gained admittance, however, his burden was still with him. After a while he came to a hill. A cross stood on top of the hill and an open tomb at the bottom. As he looked at the cross, his burden fell from his back. It rolled down the hill into the tomb.

Christian exclaimed, "He hath given me rest, by his sorrow, and life, by his death." He wept as he thought about the power of the cross to relieve him of his burden. Finally, he went on his way singing,

> Thus far did I come laden with my sin,
> Nor could ought ease the grief that I was in,
> Till I came hither: What a place is this!
> Must here be the beginning of my bliss?
> Must here the burden fall from off my back?
> Must here the strings that bound it to me crack?
> Blest cross! Blest Sepulchre! Blest rather be
> The Man that there was put to shame for me.[1]

The cross is God's way of dealing with sin. This is the consistent theme of the New Testament. Christ "died for our sins" (1 Cor.

15:3). He "was delivered over to death for our sins" (Rom. 4:25). He "has appeared once for all at the end of the ages to do away with sin by the sacrifice of himself" (Heb. 9:26). He "offered for all time one sacrifice for sins" (Heb. 10:12). "For Christ died for sins once for all, the righteous for the unrighteous, to bring you to God" (1 Pet. 3:18).

As the focal point of God's dealing with sin, the cross is the ground of forgiveness. Jesus spoke of His blood "which is poured out for many for the forgiveness of sin" (Matt. 26:28). In Christ, "we have redemption through his blood, the forgiveness of sins" (Eph. 1:7; see Col. 1:13-14). In light of this testimony, we can see why Christian's burden fell away at the cross.

Basic Factors

Several factors are evident in the New Testament presentation of the cross. Consideration of these will help to clarify our understanding.

Historical Forces and Saving Purposes

The meaning of the cross involves two dimensions. It is presented as the result of historical forces operative in Palestine in the first century AD. It is also presented as an essential part of God's purpose. *Historical forces.*—The crucifixion of Jesus was the result of a conspiracy between religious leaders and the politicians (Matt. 22:15; 27:62; Mark 12:13; John 18:3). Few people have aroused such hostility in so short a time. From the beginning of Jesus' ministry, He was opposed by powerful special-interest groups.

One source of opposition came from the Pharisees. They were primarily a religious group rather than a political party. Their members came largely from the middle class. They were genuinely pious people whose greatest concern was keeping the law. To help them apply the law to every area of life, they had developed an elaborate oral tradition. This oral law had as much authority for them as the Torah. Their chief instrument in propagating their religion was the synagogue.

In their strict adherence to the oral tradition, many of the Pharisees

had become legalistic. Religion became so preoccupied with pre-
scriptions, the heart had gone out of it. The original intent of the law
was often forgotten. This fostered a spirit of formalism and self-
righteousness.

At least three reasons can be given for Pharisaic opposition to
Jesus. First, they considered Him an imposter. As guardians of the
messianic hope, they looked forward to the promised deliverer. But
they could never accept a man who was born under the rumor of
scandal (Mark 6:1-6), who did not appreciate their values or share
their hope. The messianic hopes of Pharisees are described in the
intertestamental work, The Psalms of Solomon (ch. 17). To compare
this picture with the ministry of Jesus is to see that He did not fit.
Second, Jesus repudiated their oral tradition. He was more concerned
with the original intent behind the divine law. He told the Pharisees
that their tradition actually nullified the word of God (Matt. 15:3,6).
Third, Jesus' inclusion of all races within His care was an open rebuke to the racial and religious exclusivism of the legalists. With
Him, Samaritans (Luke 10:30 *ff*.; John 4:4 *ff*.) and Romans (Matt.
8:10), as well as Jews, found acceptance. As Jesus' popularity grew,
the Pharisees felt their influence threatened.

Another source of opposition came from the Sadducees. This
group was represented by the wealthy aristocracy and the priesthood
in Jerusalem. Most of them were priests. They had charge of the Temple and its ministry. They also constituted a majority on the Sanhedrin, the high court for Jewish affairs. Like the Pharisees, they
accepted the law of Moses. Unlike the Pharisees, however, they did
not accept the oral tradition as binding.

The Sadducees held their position and exercised their privileges by
permission of the Romans. They were extremely sensitive to any
change in the political climate. Since they had the most to lose in any
revolution, they were against any alteration of the status quo.

To this group, Jesus could only appear to be a revolutionary. They
viewed Jesus' growing movement with alarm. He threatened their
privileged position. Though the Sadducees were not often on speaking terms with Pharisees, they were willing to cooperate against a
common danger.

Still another source of opposition came from the common people. Jesus had excited their messianic expectation. Jesus' mighty works and references to a kingdom found enthusiastic acceptance. But the longer He ministered and taught, the more they realized that something was wrong. He did not fit their preconceived categories. John said, "Many of his disciples turned back and no longer followed him" (John 6:66). Some students have suggested that this was the reason Judas eventually betrayed Jesus. Judas was disappointed in the direction of Jesus' ministry.

Jesus' crucifixion was carried out with the permission of the Roman procurator. Before Pilate, the Jewish leaders charged Jesus with "subverting our nation. He opposes payment of taxes to Caesar and claims to be Christ, a king" (Luke 23:2). Pilate examined Jesus and saw through the scheme of the Jewish officials. He sought ways to release Jesus. His opinion was, "I . . . have found no basis for your charges against him" (v. 14). Pilate's wife agreed. She warned her husband, "Don't have anything to do with that *innocent man,* for I have suffered a great deal today in a dream because of him" (Matt. 27:19, author's italics). But Jesus' opponents threatened Pilate with a form of blackmail. "If you let this man go, you are no friend of Caesar. Anyone who claims to be a king opposes Caesar" (John 19:12). Pilate relented and handed Jesus over to be crucified.

What was Jesus' role in all of this? Jesus was not simply a passive victim. His words and actions led to the charge of blasphemy. He claimed to forgive sin (Mark 2:6-7), to fulfill the law (Matt. 5:17), to be greater than the Temple (Matt. 12:6), and to be Lord of the sabbath (Matt. 12:8). He believed that He had a unique relation to God (Matt. 11:27) and that the kingdom of God was present in Him (Matt. 12:28; Luke 11:20). Cleansing the Temple could not help but arouse opposition (Mark 11:12-18). A tongue-lashing such as that in Matthew 23 was not calculated to win friends among the opposition. Jesus was not content to remain on the outskirts of human affairs. He challenged the centers of power with sovereign authority. Jesus did not avoid Jerusalem even though He knew what was waiting for Him there. Luke's Gospel records that, at the proper time, "Jesus resolutely set out for Jerusalem" (9:51).

Saving purpose.—From a merely human perspective, this could be seen as deliberately courting disaster. It is true at one level that Jesus' enemies killed Him. But at a deeper level He laid down His life of His own will. "I lay down my life—only to take it up again. No one takes it from me, but I lay it down of my own accord" (John 10:17-18).

More was involved in Jesus' death, therefore, than religion and politics. Historical factors alone can never explain the cross. Jesus' death must be explained ultimately as the will of God. This is the meaning of the statements in the New Testament which speak of God as giving or sending His Son (John 3:16; Rom. 8:3,32; Gal. 4:4). It is also the meaning of passages which speak of the Son giving Himself (Gal. 2:20). The cross did not catch God by surprise. He willed it. And Jesus, the obedient Son, embraced it.

Historical forces and saving purpose are brought together in the first Christian sermon. "This man was handed over to you by God's set purpose and foreknowledge; and you, with the help of wicked men, put him to death by nailing him to the cross" (Acts 2:23; compare 1 Pet. 1:20). This view shows a complete change in Peter's understanding. Earlier he had refused to believe that the Messiah would suffer and die (Mark 8:32-33). After the resurrection he understood that the cross was neither an accident nor a tragedy. It was the way God had chosen to save the world.

Love the Righteousness

God's love.—The life and death of Christ cannot be understood apart from the love of God.[2] All that God has done for us depends on His love. This is summed up in a single statement, "God is love" (1 John 4:8). God is the source of all love. Everything He does reflects His nature as love. This is not the same thing as saying that love is God. It is important to keep the biblical order. God is the subject. Otherwise we might be tempted to judge God by our own preconceived ideas of love. God's love is always the standard by which all of our experiences of love must be evaluated.

How do we know the meaning of God's love? In an earlier chapter, we saw that God is known by what He does. His actions give us the clue to His nature. Again it is important to pay attention to the verbs (action words). After saying "God is love," John wrote, "This is how God showed his love among us: He sent his one and only Son into the world that we might have life through him" (1 John 4:9). This recalls John 3:16. "For God so loved the world that he gave his one and only Son, that whoever believes in him shall not perish but have eternal life." God's love is defined by the sending of His Son. The message of divine love is not communicated by heavenly handwriting in the sky. It takes concrete form in our midst. Christ is the reality of God's love in human flesh.

The following characteristics will help us understand this love more clearly. First, God's love is unconditional. God does not say, "I will love you if you prove worthy." Sinful people do not have to meet conditions to be loved. They are loved already.

God's unconditional love is demonstrated in Jesus' ministry. Jesus loved the unlovely. He cared for the outcasts. He fellowshipped with people we would say were from "the wrong side of the tracks." He was the friend of sinners. His love embraced the religious (Nicodemus), the immoral (the woman caught in adultery), the political revolutionaries (Zealots), dishonest businessmen (Zacchaeus), social outcasts (the Samaritan woman), and those who crucified Him ("Father forgive them, for they do not know what they are doing," Luke 23:34).

Unconditional love is also at the heart of the apostolic faith. "Christ died for the ungodly. God demonstrates his own love for us in this: While we were still sinners, Christ died for us" (Rom. 5:6,8). Two things are clear from this statement. (1) We do not deserve God's love. (2) God does not love us because Christ died for us. Rather, Christ died for us because God loves us.

Second, God's love is universal. "For God so loved the world" (John 3:16). This means that the divine concern knows no barriers. It cannot be confined by class, culture, creed, or color. A love so large can never be merely a neighborhood affair.

The universality of God's love is the basis for calling Jesus "the Savior of the world" (1 John 4:14). It also explains why God "wants all men to be saved and to come to a knowledge of the truth" (1 Tim. 2:4).

Third, God's love is self-giving. It is motivated by a desire to give rather than to get. In love, God does not give us *some thing* other than Himself. He gives Himself.

Fourth, God's love is sacrificial. God sent His Son "as an atoning sacrifice for our sins" (1 John 4:10). Divine love does not stop with the incarnation. It embraces the sacrifice of the cross. Calvary defines more clearly than anything else what it means to say, "God is love." After that event, divine love will always be fixed in our minds in the shape of a cross.

Fifth, God's love is one with Christ's love. Frequently the New Testament speaks of Christ's love for us. For example, "Christ loved us and gave himself up for us" (Eph. 5:2). "The Son of God . . . loved me and gave himself for me" (Gal. 2:20). The love of the Son is not different from the love of the Father. Just as they are one in nature and purpose, so they are one in their love for the world.

God's righteousness.—To say that God is righteous means that He is self-consistent. He always acts in accordance with His nature. He is never arbitrary. He is never "out of character" as God. Another way of saying this is to say that God is faithful. With Him "there is never the slightest variation or shadow of inconsistency" (Jas. 1:17, Phillips). Thus, God's activity in history is always a true revelation of His character.

Sometimes people speak of God's righteousness as His justice. The emphasis is that God is Judge who always does what is right. He conforms to the moral law and expects His people to conform as well. This is a true way to speak of God. But we must remember two things. First, God Himself is the standard of what is right. Second, the moral law is not an external code that is higher than God. It is a revelation of His own personal will. There is no standard greater than God.

Because God is consistent (righteous), He opposes human sinfulness. God actively resists all that opposes His purpose in the world. There is, therefore, a punitive dimension to righteousness (Amos 3:2; Rom. 6:23). This divine opposition to sin is known as the wrath of God. "The wrath of God is being revealed from heaven against all the godlessness and wickedness of men" (Rom. 1:18; see 2:5; 5:9; Eph. 5:6; Col. 3:6).

Many people find the idea of the wrath of God difficult to accept. It seems "out of character" for God. His anger seems to contradict the reality of His love. As a result, some scholars have rejected the view that God's wrath is personal. Rather, wrath is defined as the outworking of the laws of cause and effect in a moral universe. This means that the universe was created so as to uphold the moral law. When we violate this law, we suffer the inevitable consequences. Such a view may be correct in what it affirms. We do reap what we sow (Gal. 6:7). But this view is wrong in what it denies. The wrath of God in the New Testament is more than an impersonal sequence of cause and effect.

God's wrath may be defined as His personal and persistent opposition to sin. Far from contradicting His love, it may be an expression of it. He cares deeply for what is right, and He cares for His rebellious creatures. God cares so much that He will not let people get by with their sins. Not to punish would be a sign of moral indifference and lack of concern.

The wrath of God may be compared to fire. Fire can be beneficial or destructive. The way we experience it depends on our relationship to it. If we are rightly related to it, we experience light, warmth, protection. But if we are not rightly related to it, we can be burned, scarred, or consumed. The New Testament states, "God is love" (1 John 4:8). It also affirms, "Our God is a consuming fire" (Heb. 12:29). These two statements belong together. There is no contradiction.

Because God is consistent (righteous), He acts to save. In the Bible, righteousness and salvation are closely connected. In some Old Testament contexts, they are practically synonymous. For example, "I am bringing my righteousness near;/it is not far away;/and my salvation will not be delayed" (Isa. 46:13). "But my salvation will last forever,/my righteousness will never fail" (51:6). "I delight greatly in the Lord;/my soul rejoices in my God./For He has clothed me with garments of salvation/and arrayed me in a robe of righteousness" (61:10). God is described as "a righteous God and Savior" (45:21; compare Ps. 51:14).

The same relationship between righteousness and salvation is found in the New Testament. Paul emphasized that God's righteousness is revealed in the gospel (Rom. 1:17). In Christ, the righteous God acted to bring people into a right relationship with Himself (compare Rom. 3:21-31). Here righteousness refers to God's character and to His gift of righteousness (right relationship) to us.

Similarly, John emphasized the relation of the divine righteousness to the forgiveness of sins. "If we confess our sins, He is faithful and righteous to forgive our sins and to cleanse us from all unrighteousness" (1 John 1:9, NASB). The emphasis is that, because God is righteous, He is faithful to His promise to forgive penitent sinners.

The positive relation of divine righteousness to salvation is not always acknowledged in theology and preaching. Righteousness as punitive justice is often emphasized exclusively. When this is done righteousness and love are torn apart. There is also the subtle tendency to separate the Father and the Son in the work of salvation. If we are not careful, we can leave the impression that the Father is vindictive while the Son is loving. Probably no one wants to paint such a portrait. But it is a caricature we can fall into if we do not maintain the biblical balance in talking about righteousness and love. We must remember that God is loving in His righteousness and righteous in His loving. Furthermore, there is a punitive side to God's righteousness. But there is another side. God's righteousness points to His saving activity. God does not save us *in spite of* His righteousness. He saves us *because of* his righteousness.

Representation and Substitution

Our understanding of the cross is further deepened by thinking of Christ as our representative and as our substitute.

Christ our representative.—As our representative, Christ acts *on our behalf*. This strongly emphasizes His oneness with us. In His oneness with us, He does for us what we could never do. He does not stand apart from us, but involves us in His work.

An example of representation is Paul's contrast between Adam and

Christ. He developed this contrast in Romans 5:12-21 and 1 Corinthians 15:45-49. Adam and Christ represent two races of people. Adam is the head of the race of fallen persons. Sin and death came into the world through him. Because of our fallenness we are members of Adam's race. We have disobeyed God. We, too, experience sin and death.

Christ (the last Adam) represents a new race of people. These are the people who have been saved from sin. Where Adam failed, Christ succeeded. Christ is the source of life and hope. Because of our relation to Christ, we belong to this new race.

This idea is expressed in other ways. Paul wrote, "One died for all, and therefore all died" (2 Cor. 5:14). The death of the Representative involves the death of those whom He represents. Again, "Christ has been raised from the dead, the firstfruits of those who have fallen asleep" (1 Cor. 15:20). Christ's resurrection is the pledge of the resurrection of His people. They are involved in His resurrection by way of promise.

Another example of representation is the emphasis on Christ as our High Priest. This is a major theme in the Book of Hebrews. Because of Christ's oneness with us in His life and death, He represents us in the heavenly court (Heb. 9:24).

Christ our substitute.—As our substitute, Christ acted *in our place*. This goes a step beyond representation. Christ not only acted on our behalf but also took our place. This emphasis expresses more clearly the uniqueness of Jesus' suffering and death for us. It means that He experienced in our place the suffering and death we deserved.[3] A contemporary theologian, Leon Morris, testifies to the meaning of substitution in these words:

> The value of this way of viewing the atonement is its flexibility combined with its adaptability to the different ways of stating our need. Was there a price to be paid? He paid it. Was there a victory to be won? He won it. Was there a penalty to be borne? He bore it. Was there a judgment to be faced? He faced it. View man's plight how you will, the witness of the New Testament is that Christ has come where man ought to be and has met in full all the demands that might be made on man.[4]

This thought is phrased in several ways in the New Testament. Jesus spoke of giving His life "a ransom for many" (Mark 10:45). The phrase "for many" should probably be taken in a substitutionary sense. The meaning is "give his life a ransom instead of (in the place of) many." The same point is made in Peter's statement, "He himself bore our sins in his body on the tree, so that we might die to sins and live for righteousness; by his wounds you have been healed" (1 Pet. 2:24). No sentence more simply declared the meaning of the cross for the earliest Christians. The burden of sin and guilt was no longer theirs to carry. Jesus had taken it upon Himself and carried it away. Peter's words recall the Suffering Servant of Isaiah 53. There we are told that "he bore the sins of many" and "by his wounds we are healed" (v. 5).

Paul's language about the cross often involved substitution. "God made him who had no sin to be sin for us, so that in him we might become the righteousness of God" (2 Cor. 5:21). "Christ redeemed us from the curse of the law by becoming a curse for us, for it is written: 'Cursed is everyone who is hung on a tree'" (Gal. 3:13).

In thinking of Christ as substitute, we must be careful to emphasize Christ's oneness with God. This will keep us from thinking of Christ as a third party who comes between God and man who absorbs all the blows God can inflict. Rather, substitution means that in Christ God Himself bears the consequences of our sin. God saves us at great cost to Himself, not at cost to a third party. Salvation is free, but it is not cheap. The cross as substitutionary is the supreme witness to the costly nature of God's saving activity.

Biblical Images

The New Testament does not present a theory of the cross as such. The earliest Christians did not try to make the death of Jesus fit their preconceived ideas. The fact that Jesus died and rose again meant that they had to give up a lot of their earlier notions. They had to rethink the meaning of Jesus in the light of what actually happened. To do this, they took up images and pictures from everyday life to convey their understanding.

There is a variety of these images in the New Testament. They are drawn from different areas of experience. Each image tells us something important about the cross. But no one image tells us everything. They are like light flashing with varying hues from the many facets of a diamond. To see the full beauty of the gem, one must view it from different angles. So it is with the cross. Each image needs the others in order to see the whole picture.

The Cross as Ransom

A key expression of this image is Mark 10:45. "For even the Son of Man did not come to be served, but to serve, and to give his life as a ransom for many." Ransom is an image drawn from ancient economic life. It means deliverance by payment of a price. The picture is a slave market or a prison. We have lost our freedom. Our lives are forfeit. There is nothing we can do to free ourselves. But someone comes and pays the price (provides the ransom) to redeem us. In this context, Jesus is the Redeemer. He delivers people from the bondage of sin. The price He paid was His own life.

This imagery is rooted in the Old Testament. There we read about the duty of a man to redeem his kinsman who had been sold into slavery because of poverty (Lev. 25:47-55). This custom provided the prophets with language to describe God's saving work. God is designated as Israel's Redeemer. He delivered them from slavery in Egypt. He promised to deliver them from Babylonian captivity. "Then you will know that I, the Lord, am your Savior,/your Redeemer, the Mighty One of Jacob" (Isa. 60:16; compare 41:14; 43:1; 44:6; 47:4). In these passages, the emphasis is on deliverance. Little is said about the payment of a price.

In the New Testament, both the fact of deliverance and the ransom price are emphasized. This is expressed in different ways. For example, Paul wrote, "You are not your own; you were bought at a price" (1 Cor. 6:19-20; 7:23). Jesus "gave himself as a ransom for all men" (1 Tim. 2:6). He "gave himself for us to redeem us from all wickedness and to purify for himself a people that are his very own" (Titus 2:14). In Revelation, the words appear, "You are worthy to take the scroll/and to open its seals,/because you were slain,/and with your blood you purchased men for God/from every tribe and language and people and nation" (Rev. 5:9). Peter declared, "For you know that it was not with perishable things such as silver or gold that you are redeemed, . . . but with the precious blood of Christ, a lamb without blemish or defect" (1 Pet. 1:18-19). In these last two verses, the ransom image overlaps with the image of sacrifice. In all of these passages, the price paid for our deliverance is made clear. Jesus did not give something other than Himself. He gave His own life.

The ransom image, however, should not be pressed too far. In the postapostolic church, the question was raised, "If Christ paid the ransom, to whom did He pay it?" Origen (about 185-254) suggested that it was paid to the devil. Gregory of Nyssa (about 335-395) developed this idea further. He described Jesus as the bait with which a fisherman baits his hook. Satan was attracted by the sinless humanity of Christ. Like a greedy fish, Satan swallowed the bait. But he was caught by the hook of Christ's divine nature which was hidden beneath His humanity. Such a view is an error. It pushes the image far beyond the intention of the biblical writers.

The main idea of the ransom image is rescue from peril through the costly self-giving of Jesus. The New Testament never suggests that Jesus was delivered to Satan. On the contrary, "Jesus called out with a loud voice, 'Father into your hands I commit my spirit'" (Luke 23:46).

The Cross as Victory

Another image for understanding the cross comes from military life. The scene is a battlefield. God and Satan are at war over the possession of our lives. We have been carried as captives to the kingdom of darkness. Christ is the warrior of God who enters the battle to defeat evil and set us free. Though the conflict is intense, Christ is victorious in every engagement. His death is the climax of the battle. For a moment, it appeared as if He had been defeated. But through the resurrection, we see the cross as victory. The forces of evil have received a death blow from which they will never recover. As a result, God has "rescued us from the dominion of darkness and brought us into the kingdom of the Son he loves" (Col. 1:13).

There are several indications that Jesus saw His ministry as a con-

flict with evil powers. At the beginning of His ministry, Jesus won a
victory over Satan by resisting temptation (Matt. 4:1-11). He described Himself as the One who binds Satan and takes away his pos-
sessions (Mark 3:27). The exorcisms are tokens of the final triumph
of the kingdom of God over the kingdom of evil (Matt. 12:28). As a
result of these triumphs, Jesus declared, "I saw Satan fall like light-
ning from heaven" (Luke 10:18). This saying does not refer to a pre-
historic fall of Satan. It is an anticipation of his ultimate defeat. The
same meaning is found in another statement: "Now is the time for
judgment on this world; now the prince of this world will be driven
out" (John 12:31).

The victory of Christ over the evil powers is also affirmed by Paul.
He wrote that Christ "disarmed the powers and authorities" and
"made a public spectacle of them, triumphing over them by the
cross" (Col. 2:15). The "powers and authorities" are all the spiritual
forces which are in rebellion against God (compare Eph. 6:12). The
term "triumphing" was used in Paul's day to describe the victory
procession of a Roman general. After a great victory, the defeated
foes were forced to march behind the chariot of the victor. This pa-
rade demonstrated the power of the conqueror and the suppression of
his enemies. Paul used this as a picture of what God did in Christ.
The cross appeared to be a humiliating instrument of defeat, but God
used it as a means of conquest. By it He disarmed His enemies and
neutralized their power to keep us enslaved.

The victory image should not be taken to mean that Satan is equal
to God. The Bible does not teach an ultimate dualism (that is, that
there are two equally powerful and eternal principles in the universe).
God alone is the Creator and supreme Ruler. All other forces are
creaturely and dependent. They are subordinate to Him.

Christ's victory at the cross will be finalized in the future. "Yet
we do not see everything subject to him" (Heb. 2:8; compare
1 Cor. 15:25-26). This is a reminder that sin is still present and powerful in the world (Eph. 6:10-18). Here we need to remember the
illustration of D day and V-day. In the life, death, and resurrection of
Jesus, a decisive victory has been won. The tide of battle has been
turned. The consummation is certain, but it is still future.

Such imagery provides encouragement for Christian living. We live "in between the times." By faith, we participate in Christ's victory. Furthermore, the Victor who reigns at God's right hand also dwells in our hearts. Because of this we can live courageously in the present and look hopefully toward the future.

The Cross as Sacrifice

This image comes from the realm of religious life. Its background is the sacrificial system of ancient Israel. The scene is a place of worship with an altar where sacrifice is offered. A worshiper brings to a priest the finest animal from his flock or herd. The priest slays the animal and sprinkles its blood on the altar. In this way the sins of the worshiper are covered. Fellowship with God is restored.

It is not possible here to discuss in detail the sacrificial system in the Old Testament. It is sufficient to mention three basic principles. First, sacrifice was God's gift. It was not a human system devised to buy God's favor. Sacrifice was operative within the covenant relationship. As such, it was a provision of divine grace. This is a crucial point. Sinners can never provide a way to God. God initiates the restoration of fellowship between Himself and sinners. Sacrifice as God's gift is stressed in Leviticus 17:11. "For the life of a creature is in the blood, and *I have given it to you* to make atonement for yourselves on the altar" (author's italics).

Second, sacrifice was also God's requirement. It was to be offered to Him to atone for sin. In the sacrificial act, the worshiper was identified with the victim. The animal was a substitute for him. The ritual intended to impress upon the worshiper the seriousness of sin: it cost a life.[5]

Third, the sacrificial rituals were limited in value. They played an important role at one stage of God's saving activity. However, they were limited in scope. Sacrifices availed only for certain kinds of sin (Lev. 4:1,13,22,27; 5:15,17-19). There were no sacrifices for defiant sins against the covenant (Num. 15:30; Deut. 17:12). But they were also limited in power. They could not effect what they symbolized.

> Not all the blood of beasts
> On Jewish altars slain,

> Could give the guilty conscience peace,
> Or wash away the stain.[6]

So the writer of Hebrews concluded, "But those sacrifices are an annual reminder of sins, because it is impossible for the blood of bulls and goats to take away sin" (Heb. 10:3-4).

The writers of the New Testament believed that Jesus fulfilled the intention of Old Testament sacrifices. Jesus provided the reality which the sacrifices only symbolized. At the cross, God's love and judgment met in the all-sufficient sacrifice of Christ. It is not surprising, therefore, that the first Christians drew on this Old Testament resource to witness to Christ. It will be helpful here to consider some of the ways they used this imagery.

(1) Jesus is identified with the Passover lamb. Paul wrote, "For Christ, our Passover lamb, has been sacrificed" (1 Cor. 5:7). Passover was the annual feast in which the Jewish nation celebrated their deliverance from Egyptian bondage. The offering of the lamb was a reminder of God's gracious provision for them when the destroying angel passed through the land. They emerged from captivity and were constituted the people of God (Ex. 19:5-6).

For Christians, the death of Christ is also a Passover sacrifice. By it, we have experienced a new and greater exodus. We have been saved from the dominion of sin and have thereby become the people of God, the new Israel (1 Pet. 2:9-10).

(2) Jesus is the sacrifice which initiates a new covenant. "After the supper he took the cup, saying, 'This cup is the new covenant in my blood which is poured out for you'" (Luke 22:20; compare Matt. 26:18; Mark 14:24; 1 Cor. 11:25). These words of Jesus echo Exodus 24 and Jeremiah 31. When the covenant was made at Sinai, Moses sprinkled blood on the people, saying, "This is the blood of the covenant that the Lord has made with you" (Ex. 24:8). Jeremiah saw the limitations of this covenant and declared that it would be replaced with a new one (Jer. 31:31-34).

Jesus pointed to the shedding of His blood on the cross as the means of establishing the new covenant. In Christ, therefore, we experience the blessings of this new relationship. A new kind of righteousness is possible because the will of God is put within the heart. A new dimension in personal communion is opened up. Knowledge of God becomes the possession of all. Cleansing from sin becomes real at the deepest level.

(3) Jesus is associated with the sin offering. This reference is to the offering made once a year when the high priest entered the holy of holies to make atonement for sin. The author of Hebrews developed this thought by contrasting the old system to Christ. Four points call for notice. First, the rituals of the old system were performed in an earthly tabernacle. This was indicative of their temporary nature. But Christ "entered heaven itself, now to appear for us in God's presence" (9:24). This signifies the finished nature of His work (compare 1:3).

Second, in the old system the blood of animals was offered for sin. Christ, however, offered Himself. In Him, priest and sacrifice are one (9:14,25-28).

Third, the old rituals were repetitious. They were repeated year after year "as an annual reminder of sins" (10:3; compare 9:25). Christ sacrificed Himself "once for all" (9:26). There is no need to do it again. It is eternally sufficient.

Finally, the old system could not effect what it symbolized. At best, it could produce a ceremonial cleansing. But the sacrifice of Christ will "cleanse our consciences from acts that lead to death, so that we may serve the living God" (9:14).

(4) Jesus is presented as the Lamb of God. The testimony of John the Baptist was, "Look, the Lamb of God, who takes away the sin of the world!" (John 1:29; compare v. 36). Some students trace the source of this description to Isaiah 53:7, "He was led like a lamb to the slaughter,/and as a sheep before her shearers is silent,/so he did not open his mouth." Others think the reference is to the Passover lamb which plays such an important role in John's story of the passion. Still others believe it is a fusion of several Old Testament sacrifices for sin.

In the Book of Revelation, Jesus is called "Lamb of God" twenty-eight times. The thought of Jesus' sacrifice is still present. Jesus is "a Lamb, looking as if it had been slain" (5:6). All praise and honor are ascribed to "the Lamb, who was slain" (5:12). The followers of Christ are those who "have washed their robes and made them white in the blood of the Lamb" (7:14). This is a clear reference to His sacrificial death. But in Revelation, sacrifice is blended with the victory image. The One who was crucified has been resurrected and glorified (1:18). The Lamb who gave His life for our sins is "the Lord of lords and the King of kings" (17:14). As such, He alone is worthy to open the book of human destiny (5:9-14). He stands on Mount Zion and receives the praises of all the redeemed (14:1-5). He will be victorious over all His enemies (17:13-14). When the vision of the heavenly city becomes a reality, "the throne of God and the Lamb" will be in the midst of it (22:3).

This brief survey shows that sacrificial imagery is deeply rooted in the New Testament witness to Christ. It's value as a way of understanding the cross can be expressed in three ways. First, sacrifice points to the costliness of Christ's death. It is a reminder that "God so loved the world that he gave his one and only son" (John 3:16) and that the Son of God "loved me and gave himself for me" (Gal. 2:20). Second, sacrifice witnesses to the effectiveness of Christ's death. Through it, our consciences are cleansed (Heb. 9:14), our sins are forgiven (Eph. 1:7), and we share in an eternal redemption (Heb. 9:12). Third, sacrifice reminds us of the purpose of Christ's death. It is "to redeem us from all wickedness and to purify for himself a people that are his very own, eager to do what is good" (Titus 2:14).

The Cross as a Revelation of Glory

Of the Gospel writers, only John connected the death of Jesus with the manifestation of God's glory. For John the whole life of Jesus showed forth the glory of God. In that revelation, the cross occupies a unique place.[7]

Glory is one of the richest words in the vocabulary of the Bible. Its root meaning is "to be heavy." Glory indicates the worth, dignity, and honor of a person. When used of God, it refers to a revelation of God's presence in power and majesty.

Frequent references to God's glory occur in the Old Testament. During the trek from Egypt to Sinai, the Israelites "looked toward the desert and there was the glory of the Lord appearing in the cloud" (Ex. 16:10). When Moses ascended Mount Sinai to receive the tablets of the Law, "the glory of the Lord settled on [the mountain]" (Ex. 24:16). When the Tent of Meeting was completed, Moses could not enter "because the cloud had settled upon it, and the glory of the Lord filled the tabernacle" (Ex. 40:35). At the dedication of Solomon's Temple, the priests could not perform their ministry "for the glory of the Lord filled his temple" (1 Kings 8:11). In Isaiah's vision of God, the angels testified, "Holy, holy, holy is the Lord Almighty;/ the whole earth is full of his glory" (Isa. 6:3). Ezekiel's vision by the river Chebar in Babylon took the form of a being enthroned in radiant light, which he described as "the appearance of the likeness of the glory of the Lord" (Ezek. 1:28).

The meaning of *glory* is enriched in the New Testament by its application to Christ. This is natural since He is believed to be "the radiance of God's glory and the exact representation of his being" (Heb. 1:3). Usually it is to Him as the risen and exalted Lord that the word *glory* is applied. He is glorified because He has accomplished God's will and has been exalted to His right hand (Acts 2:32-36; Heb. 10:12). The risen and glorified Christ was witnessed by Stephen (Acts 7:56) and encountered by Paul on the road to Damascus (Acts 9:3-6; 22:6; 26:13). References to the coming again of Christ speak of it as a revelation of His glory. "But rejoice that you participate in the sufferings of Christ, so that you may be overjoyed when his glory is revealed" (1 Pet. 4:13; 5:1; compare Mark 13:26).

In John's Gospel, however, there is a significant shift of perspective. Divine glory is revealed in Jesus from the beginning. The evangelist looked back to the whole earthly life of the incarnate Word and declared, "We have seen his glory, the glory of the one and only Son, who came from the Father" (1:14). The miracles of Jesus are signs and those who believe in Jesus can discern the deeper meaning enshrined in them. In Cana, Jesus performed a "miraculous sign" and "thus revealed his glory" (2:11). When Lazarus became ill, Jesus explained that Lazarus's illness will not end in death. "No, it is for God's glory so that God's Son may be glorified through it" (11:4).

When Lazarus was raised, Jesus affirmed, "Did I not tell you that if you believed, you would see the glory of God?" (v. 40).

But the supreme revelation of glory is to be seen in Jesus' death on the cross. As He moved toward the cross, Jesus announced, "The hour has come for the Son of Man to be glorified" (John 12:23). The meaning of this statement is made clear in the one that follows. "I tell you the truth, unless a kernel of wheat falls to the ground and dies, it remains only a single seed. But if it dies, it produces many seeds" (v. 24).

In the upper room, Jesus told His disciples, "Now is the Son of Man glorified and God is glorified in him. If God is glorified in him, then God will glorify the Son in himself, and will glorify him at once" (13:31-32). Thus glory is connected with what seems to be its opposite—the humiliation of a cross. Just as Father and Son are one in saving purpose, so they are one in the glory they share. The glory of Jesus manifested in His death was one with the glory of the Father whose will He was doing. The same thought is expressed in John 17:1-5. The glory of which Jesus spoke was the preexistent glory He shared with the Father before creation.

Consistent with this theme is the emphasis on the cross as a "lifting up." This verb has the double meaning of "to lift up on a cross" and "to exalt." The meanings are combined in John's Gospel. "As Moses lifted up the serpent in the wilderness, so must the Son of man be lifted up" (3:14, RSV). "When you have lifted up the Son of Man, then you will know who I am" (8:28). "'But I when I am lifted up from the earth, will draw all men to myself.' He said this to show the kind of death he was going to die" (12:32-33). The thought here is not of exaltation as a reward for experiencing humiliation and death. Rather it means that Christ was exalted through His death. Divine glory was revealed in the death He died for sin.

Notes

1. John Bunyan, *The Pilgrim's Progress* (London: Constable and Co., Ltd., 1926), p. 141.

2. For a survey of the biblical teaching on God's love, see Leon Morris, *Testaments of Love: A Study of Love in the Bible* (Grand Rapids: William B. Eerdmans Publishing Co., 1981). A good theological interpretation of God's love is found in John McIntyre, *On the Love of God* (New York: Harper and Brothers Publishers, 1962).

3. On the close relationship between the representative and substitionary aspects of Christ's death see Leonard Hodgson, *The Doctrine of the Atonement* (London: Nisbet & Co. Ltd., 1951), p. 142. Compare Donald Bloesch, *Essentials of Evangelical Theology* (San Francisco: Harper and Row, Publishers, 1978), 1, pp. 148-151.

4. Leon Morris, *The Cross in the New Testament* (Grand Rapids: William B. Eerdmans Publishing Co., 1965), pp. 405-406.

5. William Sanford LaSor, David Allen Hubbard, and Frederick William Bush, *Old Testament Survey: The Message, Form and Background of the Old Testament* (Grand Rapids: William B. Eerdmans Publishing Co., 1982), pp. 152-155. Compare R. J. Thompson, "Sacrifice in the Old Testament," *The Illustrated Bible Dictionary,* J. D. Douglas, ed. (Wheaton, Illinois: Tyndale House Publishers, 1980), 3, pp. 1358-1366.

6. Isaac Watts, "Not all the Blood of Beasts," Selma L. Bishop, *Isaac Watts: Hymns and Spiritual Songs* (London: Faith Press, 1962), p. 313.

7. Stephen Smalley, *John: Evangelist and Interpreter* (Exeter: The Paternoster Press, 1978), pp. 220-223.

Bibliography

Aulén, Gustav. *Christus Victor*. Translated by A. G. Herbert. London: SPCK, 1931.

Conner, W. T. *The Cross in the New Testament*. Nashville: Broadman Press, 1954.

Dale, R. W. *The Atonement*. London: Congregational Union of London and Wales, 1899.

Denney, James. *The Death of Christ*. London: Hodder and Stoughton, 1911.

Dillistone, F. W. *The Christian Understanding of Atonement*. Philadelphia: The Westminster Press, 1968.

Forsyth, P. T. *The Cruciality of the Cross*. London: Hodder and Stoughton, 1909.

Green, Michael. *The Empty Cross of Jesus*. Downer's Grove, Illinois: InterVarsity Press, 1984.

Hunt, W. Boyd. "Atonement." *Encyclopedia of Southern Baptists,* 1. Edited by Norman Wade Cox. Nashville: Broadman Press, 1958.

Kelly, John N. D. *Aspects of the Passion*. London: Mowbray, 1985.

Stewart, James S. *A Faith to Proclaim*. New York: Charles Scribners Sons, 1953.

Taylor, Vincent. *The Atonement in New Testament Teaching*. London: The Epworth Press, 1950.

Wallace, Ronald. *The Atoning Death of Christ*. Westchester, Illinois: Crossway Books, 1981.

Zahl, Paul F. M. *Who Will Deliver Us?* New York: The Seabury Press, 1983.

5

Divine Provision: Resurrection and Ascension

The eminent British preacher, R. W. Dale, said that the most life-changing experience of his ministry occurred when he discovered that Jesus was really alive. He was preparing a sermon for Easter when the thought of the risen Lord broke in upon him afresh. He related his experience in the following way:

> "Christ is alive," I said to myself; "alive! and then I paused;—alive! and then I paused again; alive! Can that really be true? living as really as I myself am? I got up and walked about repeating 'Christ is living!' 'Christ is living!' At first it seemed strange and hardly true, but at last it came upon me as a burst of sudden glory; yes, Christ is living. It was to me a new discovery. I thought that all along I had believed it; but not until that moment did I feel sure about it. I then said, 'My people shall know it; I shall preach about it again and again until they believe it as I do now.'"[1]

As a result of this experience the custom began in his church of singing an Easter hymn every Sunday morning.

Beyond doubt the resurrection of Jesus is indispensable for Christian faith. Chronologically, of course, it follows the crucifixion. But theologically it is the starting point for each writer in the New Testament. For them it was the key that unlocked the meaning of Jesus' life and ministry. Through the resurrection, they came to understand His true identify, as well as the meaning of the cross. It would not be amiss on occasion to read the Gospels backwards. For through the resurrection, we begin to understand all that preceded it.

96

The Importance of the Resurrection

How important is the resurrection for faith in Christ? Isn't it enough to believe that Christ died for our sins? Must we also believe that He has been raised from the dead? What difference does it make?

For the first Christian community, the resurrection of Christ was absolutely essential. Christ's resurrection made Christian faith possible. It was as vital a part of God's saving activity as the incarnation and the cross. "If you confess with your mouth, 'Jesus is Lord,' and believe in your heart that God raised him from the dead, you will be saved" (Rom. 10:9). The lordship of Christ which is central to salvation was acknowledged and confessed as a result of His resurrection.

The significance of the resurrection for faith is spelled out in 1 Corinthians 15:12-19.

> But if it is preached that Christ has been raised from the dead, how can some of you say that there is no resurrection of the dead? If there is no resurrection of the dead, then not even Christ has been raised. And if Christ has not been raised, our preaching is useless and so is your faith. More than that, we are then found to be false witnesses about God, for we have testified about God that he raised Christ from the dead. But he did not raise him if in fact the dead are not raised. For if the dead are not raised, then Christ has not been raised either. And if Christ has not been raised, your faith is futile; you are still in your sins. Then those also who have fallen asleep in Christ are lost. If only for this life we have hope in Christ, we are to be pitied more than all men.

This statement could be entitled "Beliefs Have Consequences." Evidently some people in the Corinthian church were playing with ideas which impugned the resurrection of Jesus. We do not know the exact nature of their belief. That it involved denial of resurrection is clear. For Paul any denial of resurrection implied denial of the resurrection of Christ. For the sake of argument, he assumed their premise and pushed it to its logical conclusion. What are the results for faith if Christ had not been raised?

(1) Preaching and faith are useless (v. 14.). Preaching here refers

to the content rather than to the act of proclamation. The word translated "useless" means "empty" or "without content." If Christ has not been raised, there is nothing to preach. Faith in the New Testament is trust in the risen Lord. But if preaching is empty, so is the faith it elicits.

(2) God is misrepresented (v. 15). The integrity of the Christian witness is at stake. We perjure ourselves if we say that God did something which He did not really do. Phillip's translation brings out the meaning. "It would mean that we are lying in our witness to God, for we have given solemn testimony that he did raise up Christ—and that would be utterly false if it should be true that the dead do not, in fact, rise again!"

(3) Sin is not overcome (v. 17). These words sound the death knell of Christian experience. The crux of this experience is the forgiveness of sins and the gift of eternal life. The heart of the gospel is that "Christ died for our sins" (1 Cor. 15:3) and "that He was raised for our justification" (Rom. 4:25). But if Christ is not risen, He is not the Savior. Forgiveness is a mirage. There is no solution to the problem of sin.

(4) Those who have fallen asleep are lost (v. 18). "Fallen asleep" is a reference to death. To fall asleep "in Christ" means to die trusting Him. Christian hope for the future is inseparably linked to Christ. Thus, Paul said with confidence, "For to me, to live is Christ and to die is gain" (Phil. 1:21). But such confidence is well-founded only if Christ is alive.

(5) We are to be pitied more than all men (v. 19). What makes Christians so pitiable is that they have given themselves to a hope that has no chance of fulfillment. Christian hope gives meaning to this life and promise of fulfillment in the life to come. If Christ is dead, however, there is no fulfillment beyond this life. All hope stops at the grave.

In summary, if Christ is not alive, there is no Christianity. God's saving purpose is at an end.

Having pushed the logic of denying the resurrection to its tragic end, Paul reversed directions: "But in fact Christ has been raised from the dead" (v. 20, RSV). Because this is true, all of the negative possibilities are reversed. Preaching is not empty. Faith is not futile. We are not false witnesses in testifying to God's saving activity. Sin is forgiven in Christ. Christians who have died are with the Lord. Here is the remarkable truth of Christian faith. It is not the worship of a dead hero. It is not following the example or teachings of an ancient sage. It is fellowship with a living Lord.

The Reality of the Resurrection

The Empty Tomb

The fact of the empty tomb.—The empty tomb of Jesus is a crucial witness to His resurrection. It is mentioned in all four Gospels (Mark 16:1-8; Matt. 28:11-15; Luke 24:1-12; John 20:11-18). It is implied in two statements in Acts. The first is "seeing what was ahead, he spoke of the resurrection of the Christ, that he was not abandoned to the grave, nor did his body see decay" (2:31). The second is, "they took him down from the tree and laid him in a tomb, but God raised him from the dead" (13:29-30). Though Paul did not mention the empty tomb, he assumed it. He wrote, "Christ died for our sins . . . he was buried . . . he was raised on the third day" (1 Cor. 15:3-4). The references to burial emphasizes the certainty of Jesus' death and thereby highlights the reality of His resurrection. Given Paul's understanding of the nature of resurrection, these words would not make sense if the tomb were not empty.

A brief look at the sequence of events from the cross to the discovery of the empty tomb will provide historical perspective on this point. Following the crucifixion, Joseph of Arimathea asked for the body of Jesus so that he could bury it. Joseph is described as a member of the Sanhedrin who opposed the action of the council in condemning Jesus (Luke 23:51). He is also depicted as one "who was himself waiting for the kingdom of God" (Mark 15:43), "a good and upright man" (Luke 23:50), and "a disciple of Jesus, but secretly because he feared the Jews" (John 19:38). His companion in the burial venture was Nicodemus (v. 39; compare 3:1-2; 7:50).

Since Joseph was a Jewish leader of some prominence, he had access to the Roman authorities in Jerusalem. Pilate granted his request

after summoning a centurion to be sure that Jesus was really dead
(Mark 15:44). It was not unusual for victims of crucifixion to live two
or three days before dying. The release of the body of a person condemned for treason to one who was not a relative was unusual, however. This may confirm the fact that Pilate did not really believe the
charges which the religious leaders brought against Jesus (Luke 23:4,
14-15).

Jesus was buried in a rock-hewn tomb belonging to Joseph (Matt.
27:60). It was near the site of the crucifixion (John 19:41). The body
of Jesus was wrapped in strips of linen with spices sprinkled between
the folds to combat the odor of decay. Nicodemus is said to have
brought an unusually large amount of myrrh and aloes (John 19:39).
The use of expensive spices in such great quantity suggests that these
two disciples wanted to pay tribute to Jesus as a king.[2] To them Jesus
was in reality what the inscription on the cross proclaimed Him to be
in derision—"The King of the Jews" (v. 19). When the preparation of
the body of Jesus was completed, a large stone was rolled across the
entrance to the tomb (Mark 15:46).

At this point, Matthew's Gospel provides a fascinating glimpse into
the activities of the Jewish authorities. Though they knew that Jesus
was dead, they were still uneasy. They went to Pilate and requested
that a guard be posted at the tomb and that the stone be sealed as an
extra measure of precaution. They reasoned that Jesus' disciples
"may come and steal the body and tell the people that he had been
raised from the dead. This last deception will be greater than the
first" (Matt. 27:64).

On the first day of the week, the day after the sabbath, Mary Magdalene and another Mary came to the tomb. Matthew tells us of an
earthquake and the descent of an angel who rolled away the stone. He
invited the women to inspect the tomb and told them that Jesus was
alive. The guards were so afraid of the angel that "they shook and
became like dead men" (Matt. 28:4).

Thus, the Jewish authorities, as well as Jesus' disciples, were aware
of the empty tomb. But they were poles apart in their reactions. The
disciples declared that Jesus was alive. God had raised Him from the
dead. The authorities, on the other hand, bribed the soldiers telling

them, "You are to say, 'His disciples came during the night and stole him away while we were asleep.' If this report gets to the governor, we will satisfy him and keep you out of trouble. So the soldiers took the money and did as they were instructed" (Matt. 28:13-15).

The function of the empty tomb.—How are we to assess the value of the empty tomb as a witness to the resurrection? To this question a threefold response can be made.

(1) The empty tomb by itself cannot be the primary basis for faith in the resurrection. A tomb can be empty for different reasons. If we found an open grave and an empty casket in a cemetary, this would not in itself be proof of resurrection. We need a true interpretation of the facts if their real significance is to be known. Apart from interpretation any fact remains ambiguous. This gives us a clue to the meaning of biblical revelation. Revelation involves event plus interpretation. The Bible does not simply catalog facts. It records a series of events which are interpreted as God's saving activity in history. For example, the New Testament does not say, "Jesus died," and leave it at that. Rather, it affirms, "Jesus *Christ, the Son of God,* died *for our sins.*" Event and interpretation are combined.

The same thing is true of the empty tomb. God did not leave its meaning up for grabs. He provided us with the proper understanding. This is the function of the angelic messenger in the story. He explained why the tomb was empty. "The angel said to the women, 'Do not be afraid, for I know that you are looking for Jesus who was crucified. He is not here; he has risen, just as he said. Come and see the place where he lay. Then go quickly, and tell his disciples: He has risen from the dead'" (Matt. 28:5-7; compare Mark 16:5-7; Luke 24:4-8).

Even so, the tomb did not lead invariably to belief in the resurrection.[3] The women who discovered the tomb seemed more perplexed than convinced (Mark 16:8; Luke 24:2). When the disciples heard their report, "they did not believe the women, because their words seemed to them like nonsense" (Luke 24:11). Peter himself ran to the tomb, found it empty, and went away "wondering to himself what had happened" (v. 12). Two disciples on the road to Emmaus heard the report but were not sure what to make of it (vv. 22-24). In one instance, the empty tomb aroused fear that the body of Jesus had been stolen or removed for some other reason (John 20:11-15). It would only be after actually meeting the risen Christ that they would know the truth of the matter for sure.

(2) If the empty tomb is not the primary basis for faith in the resurrection, it is nevertheless a strong encouragement to faith. The first followers of Jesus proclaimed the resurrection of Jesus in the same city where He had been crucified and buried. In his first sermon, Peter declared that God raised Jesus from the dead "freeing him from the agony of death, because it was impossible for death to keep its hold on him" (Acts 2:24). Again, "God has raised this Jesus to life, and we are all witnesses of the fact" (v. 32). To the authorities, the same apostle stated, "You killed the author of life, but God raised him from the dead. We are witnesses of this" (3:15; compare 4:10).

If Jesus' body had remained in the tomb, however, no amount of persuasion would have convinced the Jews that Jesus was alive. The Christian movement would not have developed as it did. If Jesus' opponents could have produced His body, Christian preaching would have been discredited from the beginning.

(3) The empty tomb is a witness to the historical and bodily nature of the resurrection. When the New Testament speaks of the resurrection of Jesus, it does not mean that God preserved the "spirit" of Jesus though His body decayed. Still less does it mean that the influence of Jesus was raised to new importance in the lives of His followers. A bodiless resurrection, or the idea that a person could be raised "spiritually" while his body decayed in a tomb would have seemed absurd to the Jews. The resurrection means that God raised the person of Jesus in His bodily existence. He was raised to a transformed kind of existence, but it was bodily, nevertheless. To say that this happened in history is to affirm that it had a basis in factual occurrence.

For this reason the empty tomb cannot be regarded as unimportant or irrelevant. We are reminded that it is an "expression of the Easter message's concern with the concrete, bodily resurrection, and at the same time a safeguard against every spiritualizing tendency to evaporate the central declarations of the resurrection. To that extent it is by no means a matter of indifference whether theology takes the empty tomb seriously.''[4]

The Resurrection Appearances

No one actually saw Jesus rise from the dead. But the reality of the event is attested by Jesus' numerous appearances.

The significance of the appearances.—Luke informed us that between the resurrection and ascension, Jesus "showed himself" to the apostles and "gave many convincing proofs that he was alive. He appeared to them over a period of forty days and spoke about the kingdom of God" (Acts 1:3). This comment gives valuable insight into the importance of the appearances.

(1) The appearances convinced the followers of Jesus that He was really alive. What the empty tomb could not achieve alone was accomplished by a series of personal encounters with the risen Jesus. The appearances took place over a period of forty days. This does not mean that Jesus was with His disciples continuously for forty days. Rather He made Himself known to them at intervals during this time.

Notice how Luke stressed the reality of the resurrection by the use of repetition: "He showed himself," "He appeared to them." He also speaks of "proofs." This word is used only here in the New Testament. It undergirds the fact that Jesus left His followers with the unshakable conviction that He was alive.

To say that "He appeared" to His followers means that He allowed them to see Him. The initiative was always His. By means of some word (Matt. 28:9; John 20:16, 19, 26) or action (Luke 24:30-31, 39-43; John 20:20, 27; 21:6, 13), He established His identity. Once He was recognized, the characteristic response was, "It is the Lord!" (John 21:7). For example, Mary Magdalene reported to the disciples, "I have seen the Lord!" (John 20:18). Two disciples who walked with Jesus on the road to Emmaus "found the Eleven and those with them, assembled together and saying, 'It is true! The Lord has risen and has appeared to Simon.' Then the two told what had happened on the way, and how Jesus was recognized by them when he broke the bread" (Luke 24:34-35). When Jesus appeared to the disciples meeting behind closed doors "for fear of the Jews," they "were overjoyed when they saw the Lord" (John 20:19-20). They reported to Thomas "that they had seen the Lord" (v. 25). When Thomas met the risen Christ, his remarkable confession was, "My Lord and my God" (v. 28).

(2) The appearances also emphasize the identify and continuity of the earthly Jesus with the risen Christ. He whom the disciples encountered in the appearances is the One who had been crucified and buried. He is the same Jesus of Nazareth whom they had followed previously. The purpose of stressing the "physical" aspects of Jesus' resurrection body was to place His identity beyond dispute. On one occasion, when Jesus appeared to His disciples, they were frightened, "thinking they saw a ghost. He said to them, 'Why are you troubled, and why do doubts rise in your minds? Look at my hands and my feet. *It is I myself!* Touch me and see; a ghost does not have flesh and bones, as you see I have" (Luke 24:37-39, author's italics; compare John 20:27).

This emphasis on identity and continuity extends beyond the resurrection narratives. It is an essential element in the New Testament witness to Christ. "Jesus of Nazareth was a man accredited by God to you. . . . and you, with the help of wicked men, put him to death by nailing him to the cross. But God raised him from the dead" (Acts 2:22-24). "The God of our fathers raised Jesus from the dead—whom you had killed by hanging him on a tree. God exalted him to his own right hand as Prince and Savior" (Acts 5:30-31). "Christ Jesus, who died—more than that, who was raised to life—is at the right hand of God" (Rom. 8:34). "But we see Jesus, who was made a little lower than the angels, now crowned with glory and honor" (Heb. 2:9). The risen and glorified Christ is the same One who was dead but is "alive for ever and ever!" (Rev. 1:18). The Lord who will return in the future is none other than "this same Jesus" (Acts 1:11). This relationship of risen glory to the suffering and death of Jesus is another factor (along with the incarnation) which grounds biblical faith in history.

(3) Furthermore, the appearances gave Jesus the opportunity to continue instructing the disciples (Acts 1:2). Before the resurrection, they had difficulty understanding what He told them. Jesus' words did not fit their preconceived notions. Even after acknowledging Jesus as the Messiah, Peter argued about the necessity of His death (Matt.

16:22-23). When Jesus spoke about His death and resurrection, they were perplexed (Mark 9:30-32).

The reality of the cross and resurrection, however, provided a new perspective. Looking back on Jesus' words and deeds, they began to understand more clearly (compare John 2:22; 12:16). His continued teaching helped to erase many of their question marks. After Jesus returned to the Father, the Holy Spirit continued to lead them into an even greater comprehension (John 14:26; 15:26; 16:12-15).

The subject of Jesus' teaching was the kingdom of God (Acts 1:3). This is the theme that dominated His message before the cross. He was now able to help them integrate this with His death and resurrection. An example of Jesus' postresurrection instruction is given in Luke 24:27. "Beginning with Moses and the Prophets, he explained to them what was said in all the Scriptures concerning himself." We may infer that the topics Jesus and the disciples discussed were (a) the reality and nature of Jesus' messiahship, (b) how He fulfilled the Old Testament promise of salvation, and (c) their role as witnesses of these events. These three themes form the content of Christian preaching as we know it from Acts and the Epistles.

The people to whom He appeared.—It is often said that Jesus only appeared to those who believed that He was the Messiah, the Son of God. Certainly He did not appear to Pilate, Herod, or to any of His enemies in the Sanhedrin. Nor did He make Himself known to the curious public. But was belief in Him a prerequisite in every appearance? There seem to be at least two exceptions.

One possible exception is James. In John 7:5 we read, "For even his own brothers did not believe in him." It was not until after the resurrection that they are found among Jesus' followers (Acts 1:14). The appearance to James (1 Cor. 15:7) was probably the occasion of his conversion and the key factor that led the others to belief.

The second exception is Paul. He was a Pharisee who opposed the Christian faith from its beginning. Not only was he instrumental in the death of Stephen (Acts 7:58-60) but "[he] began to destroy the church. Going from house to house, he dragged off men and women and put them in prison" (Acts 8:3). On a trip to Damascus, Paul encountered the risen Christ and was converted (Acts 9:3-7; 22:6-11;

26:12-16). This experience took place after Jesus' ascension and exaltation to the right hand of God. Nevertheless, Paul interpreted it as a resurrection appearance as real and valid as those that took place before the ascension. "And last of all, as to one born abnormally late, he appeared even to me!" (1 Cor. 15:8, Phillips).

The ones to whom Jesus appeared were chosen beforehand to be witnesses to the reality of the resurrection (Acts 10:41). Once again we confront the twin themes of election and responsibility. As God chose Abraham, Moses, and the prophets to witness to the promise of salvation, so He chose apostles to witness to the fulfillment of salvation in Christ. "He commanded us to preach to the people and to testify that he is the one whom God appointed as judge of the living and the dead. All the prophets testify about him that everyone who believes in him receives forgiveness of sins through his name" (Acts 10:42-43).

The Resurrection Body of Jesus

A distinctive emphasis.—That the New Testament emphasizes the resurrection body of Jesus is significant. It distinguishes biblical faith from certain streams of Greek philosophy. In the Greek tradition, for example, there is a strong emphasis on the immortality of the soul. The soul is thought to be immortal in and of itself. There is a tendency to minimize the significance of the body. The result is a dualism in which body and soul are thought of as two different substances. At best, the body is a hindrance to the soul. At worst, it is the soul's prison. In this view, salvation is the release of the soul from the body. The ideal is bodiless existence in the eternal sphere.

Paul met this kind of thought when he preached in Athens. He declared that God "has set a day when he will judge the world with justice by the man he has appointed. He has given proof of this to all men by raising him from the dead" (Acts 17:31). Paul might have received a more favorable hearing if he had preached the traditional Greek view of immortality. But to omit the resurrection with its implications for bodily existence would have compromised the uniqueness of the Christian message. How did the majority of Athenians receive Paul's words? "When they heard about the resurrection of the dead, *some of them sneered,* but others said, 'We want to hear you again on this subject'" (Acts 17:32, author's italics).

In biblical faith, bodily existence is not depreciated. It is the form God gave us in creation. The body is not thought of as a husk to be peeled off at death. It is not a hindrance to the soul, nor is it inherently evil. The body can be used for evil purposes but it can also be dedicated to God as an instrument of righteousness (Rom. 12:1; 1 Cor. 6:12-20). Salvation in this view is not the separation of the soul from the body but the transformation of the whole person into the likeness of Christ. The ideal is not bodiless existence but eternal fellowship with Christ in a glorified bodily existence.

A glorified existence.—The appearances of Jesus in bodily form convinced the disciples of His identity. The risen Lord was, indeed, Jesus of Nazareth who had been crucified. Within this continuity, however, there was an element of discontinuity. The body of Jesus had been glorified by the resurrection. He was no longer bound by the limitations of time and space. He could pass through closed doors (John 20:19,26). He could appear instantaneously at the place and time of His choosing (Luke 24:36; John 20:19). He could pass through a sealed tomb (implied in Matt. 28:2,6). This tells us why the stone was rolled away from the tomb. It was not to let Jesus out but to let His followers in. He had no need to be let out. The tomb could not hold Him.

The grave clothes offer another interesting illustration of this point. John's Gospel records that Peter and another disciple ran to the empty tomb. Peter "saw the strips of linen lying there, as well as the burial cloth that had been around Jesus' head. The cloth was folded by itself, separate from the linen" (John 20:7). If the body of Jesus had been stolen, by enemies or friends, they probably would not have unwrapped the body. The presence and form of the wrappings suggest that Jesus' body simply passed through them. The transformation of His body meant that He could pass through any material barriers. The uniqueness of this resurrection contrasts clearly with Lazarus. When Jesus called him back to life he came out of the tomb "his hands and feet wrapped with strips of linen, and a cloth around his face" (John 11:44).

Though no longer limited by materiality, Jesus could interact with it. He was not a ghost (Luke 24:39). He could be seen with the eyes (John 20:20,29; Acts 1:9), heard with the ears (John 20:16), and touched with the hands (Matt. 28:9; Luke 24:39; John 20:27). He still had the scars from His crucifixion. He ate food and enjoyed table fellowship with His friends (Luke 24:41-43; John 21:12-13; Acts 1:4; compare 10:41).

The resurrection body of Jesus indicates that He belongs to the new creation. This means that His resurrection is not one of a class; it is unique. It differs "in kind" from other instances of being raised in the New Testament. During His ministry, Jesus raised to life the son of the widow of Nain (Luke 7:11-16), Jairus' daughter (Luke 8:49-56), and Lazarus (John 11:32-44). These miracles anticipate the deliverance of the body in the future. In each instance, however, the person was restored to the conditions of life in the present age. They were not transformed. Death was not overcome. It was merely postponed.

But the resurrection of Jesus was different. He was raised to a new order of existence. He triumphed over death. He was raised never to die again.

The Transformation of the Disciples

Between the crucifixion and the day of Pentecost, a radical transformation took place in the lives of the disciples. The same men who met "with the doors locked for fear of the Jews" (John 20:19) became the nucleus of a group which "turned the world upside down" (Acts 17:6, KJV). Neither imprisonment nor the threat of death intimidated them. They gave their lives for the proclamation of the gospel.

Representative of this change in attitude is Simon Peter. He had followed Jesus with an eager but blundering loyalty. He confessed that Jesus was the Messiah but argued with Him about its meaning (Matt. 16:22). He exuded a willingness to lay down his life for Jesus (John 13:37) and even drew a sword in Jesus' defense (John 18:10). After all of this, however, he denied having any connection with Jesus. "He began to call curses on himself, and he swore to them, 'I don't know this man you are talking about'" (Mark 14:71).

After the resurrection, however, Peter had new courage. He confronted the Jewish authorities with the truth of Jesus' messiahship and resurrection. They responded by putting him in jail (Acts 4:3) and commanding him "not to speak or teach at all in the name of Jesus" (v. 18). Peter replied, "Judge for yourselves whether it is right in God's sight to obey you rather than God. For we cannot help speaking about what we have seen and heard" (vv. 19-20). A similar scene is enacted in Acts 5. After being warned by the authorities, "The apostles left the Sanhedrin, rejoicing because that had been counted worthy of suffering for the Name. Day after day, in the temple courts and from house to house, they never stopped teaching and proclaiming the good news that Jesus is the Christ" (vv. 41-42).

How can we most adequately account for such a transformation? There is nothing in their previous experience to account for the change. In all probability, they would have eventually disbanded. There was really nothing to hold them together. The difference, therefore, did not result from a gradual recovery from disappointment. It can only be attributed to the fact that Jesus had risen and poured out His Spirit on them.

The Implications of the Resurrection

The Vindication of Christ

To vindicate means "to show to be right." To speak of the vindication of Jesus means that He was shown to be right in all that He said and did. God vindicated Jesus by raising Him from the dead. The resurrection, therefore, was God's way of reversing the world's false estimate of Jesus. This theme is prominent in Acts. It is seen in the repeated contrasts between the way the world treated Jesus and the way God treated Him. "You killed him . . . but God raised Him from the dead" (Acts 2:23-24; 3:15; 4:10; 5:30; 10:39-40; 13:29-40).

During Jesus' earthly ministry, His messianic status was denied. He was rejected, condemned, and crucified as a criminal. By raising Him from the dead, however, God has shown Him to be "both Lord and Christ" (Acts 2:36). Jesus was treated by the world as unrighteous. By the resurrection, He has been revealed as "the Holy and Righteous One" (Acts 3:14). The one who was thought to be a messianic pretender has been exalted as "Prince and Savior" (Acts 5:31). Thus, the resurrection was God's yes to the ministry of His Son. It certified that Jesus' obedience was complete, His messianic claims were true, and His death for sin was effective.

The Basis of Resurrection Hope

The resurrection of Jesus carries with it the promise of resurrection for all who belong to Him. Our own destiny is integrally related to His. He is described as "the firstborn from among the dead" (Col. 1:18) and "the firstfruits of those who have fallen asleep" (1 Cor. 15:20). The word "firstfruits" is an agricultural metaphor. Its background is Leviticus 23:4-11. During the Passover, the first sheaf of grain was presented to the Lord. It served as a promise of a larger harvest to follow. So with Christ. He was the first to be raised from the dead. His resurrection, therefore, is the promise of the resurrection of all who are in Him.

Notice the different ways this hope is expressed. "If we have been united with him in his death, we will certainly be united with him in his resurrection" (Rom. 6:5). "And if the Spirit of him who raised Jesus from the dead is living in you, he who raised Christ from the dead will also give life to your mortal bodies through his Spirit who lives in you" (Rom. 8:11). "By his power God raised the Lord from the dead, and he will raise us also" (1 Cor. 6:14).

The Defeat of Death

Death is portrayed as the enemy of humanity (1 Cor. 15:26). This is because of its relation to sin (Rom. 6:23; 1 Cor. 15:56). It has the power to intimidate through fear (Heb. 2:15) and to separate us from God (Rev. 21:8). (Compare ch. 1 on death as a consequence of sin.)

In His resurrection, however, Jesus did not merely survive death. He conquered it. As Paul expressed it, Christ "has destroyed death and has brought life and immortality to light" (2 Tim. 1:10). How has He done this? First, He has defeated the one who has the power of death, for example, the devil (Heb. 2:14). Second, He has broken the power of sin from which death gets its sting (1 Cor. 15:55-56). Third, He has granted to us the life of the new age, eternal life, which death cannot overcome (John 11:25; Rom. 8:11). Of this life James Denney has written,

> Only *one* life has ever won the victory over death: only one kind of life can ever win it—that kind which was in Him, which *is* in Him, which He shares with all whom faith makes one with Him. That is our hope, to be really members of Christ, living with a life which comes from God and has already vanquished death. God has given us eternal life, and this life is in His Son.[5]

This does not mean, of course, that death is no longer real. In affirming Christ's victory, there is no place for naiveté about the pain death inflicts in this present age. "It is appointed for men to die once" (Heb. 9:27, RSV). We know only too well that death frequently leaves in its path broken hearts, unfulfilled dreams, and acute loneliness. Christians are not spared the grief process. We are not promised that we will never experience sorrow. We are encouraged, however, not "to grieve like the rest of men, who have no hope" (1 Thess. 4:13). Because of the resurrection, we have the assurance that death can never frustrate God's purpose for our lives nor separate us from Him (Rom. 8:28,35-39).

The Ascension

The Fact of the Ascension

The ascension of Jesus refers to His return to heaven. At the conclusion of His earthly ministry, He entered the eternal dimension from which He came (compare John 6:62; 20:17). The only description of the event is given by Luke in Acts 1.[6] It does not picture the actual entrance of Jesus into heaven. It is rather a departure scene described from the standpoint of the disciples.

> So when they met together, they asked him, "Lord, are you at this time going to restore the kingdom to Israel?" He said to them: "It is not for you to know the times or dates the Father has set by his own authority. But you will receive power when the Holy Spirit comes on you; and you will be my witnesses in Jerusalem, and in all Judea and Samaria, and to the ends of the earth." After he said this, he was taken up before their eyes, and a cloud hid him from their sight. They were looking

intently up into the sky as he was going, when suddenly two men dressed in white stood beside them. "Men of Galilee," they said, "Why do you stand here looking into the sky? This same Jesus, who has been taken from you into heaven, will come back in the same way you have seen him go into heaven" (Acts 1:6-11).

The ascension represents a transition from one stage of God's saving activity to another. It is the necessary prelude to the coming of the Holy Spirit, the mission of the church, and the consummation (Acts 3:21). But we must not think that because Jesus is no longer present in bodily form He is no longer active. His ascension does not mean that He has retired to the sidelines. Notice how Luke began the Acts: "In my former book, Theophilus, I wrote about all that Jesus *began* to do and to teach" (1:1, author's italics). He is still active, but in a different way.

The Implications of the Ascension

The exaltation of Jesus.—The ascension of Jesus involves His exaltation to the right hand of God (Acts 2:31; 5:30). The phrase "right hand of God" is common in the Epistles as a designation of the status which Jesus has as a result of His resurrection and ascension.[7] For example, Paul wrote that "Christ Jesus, who died—more than that, who was raised to life—is at the right hand of God and is also interceding for us" (Rom. 8:34). God "raised him from the dead and seated him at his right hand in the heavenly realms" (Eph. 1:20; compare Col. 3:1). The writer of Hebrews declared that after Jesus "had provided purification for sins, he sat down at the right hand of the Majesty in heaven" (Heb. 1:3; compare 8:1; 10:12; 12:2). Peter spoke of "Jesus Christ, who has gone into heaven, and is at God's right hand" (1 Pet. 3:22).

How are we to understand the phrase? It is not an attempt to map the geography of heaven. Rather, it is a metaphor for a position of glory, honor, and power. To speak of Jesus in this way means that He occupies the highest position in the universe. He has been enthroned as the ruler of the cosmos (Matt. 28:18; Eph. 1:21-22; Heb. 2:8; 1 Pet. 3:22).

Another way of saying this is to declare, "He reigns! He is Lord!"

The kingdom of God which was manifested in Jesus' historical ministry continues. In Christ, God is already victorious over all that opposes Him. The power of His kingdom is present. We can experience His lordship and participate in His victory now.[8]

Even so, evil is still rampant. As in the case of death, there is no place for naiveté about the presence and power of sin. The struggle is real. The New Testament recognizes this tension between the "already" and the "not yet." "In putting everything under him, God left nothing that is not subject to him. *Yet at present we do not see everything subject to him*" (Heb. 2:8, author's italics). "For he must reign *until he has put all* [*things*] *under his feet*" (1 Cor. 15:25, author's italics). For this reason, the New Testament has a strong emphasis on the future. Our experience of Christ's rule, therefore, is real but incomplete. The full manifestation of the kingdom is in the future.

The lordship of Jesus.—By virtue of His exaltation, Jesus is acknowledged as Lord (Eph. 1:20-23). The confession of Jesus' lordship is the completion of a movement that began with the incarnation. In that event, "the Word became flesh" (John 1:14). (Compare ch. 3 on the meaning of the incarnation.) The Son of God became a servant and was "obedient to death—even death on a cross" (Phil. 2:8). As a result "God exalted him to the highest place and gave him the name that is above every name, that at the name of Jesus every knee should bow, in heaven and on earth, and every tongue confess that Jesus is Lord, to the glory of God the Father" (vv. 9-11).

The name given to Jesus is "Lord." This is a remarkable designation. In one sense it refers to His present rule. But there is more to it than that. It points to the deity of Christ.

The word "Lord" (*kurios*) is used in the Greek translation of the Old Testament (the Septuagint) to render the Hebrew name of God (Yahweh). Paul was familiar with this Greek translation and quoted from it frequently. In addition, he took passages from the Old Testament in which "Lord" clearly applied to Yahweh and applied them to Christ (Rom. 10:13 = Joel 2:32). The confession of Jesus' lordship is involved in the meaning of salvation (Rom. 10:9). This confession can only be made with the help of the Holy Spirit (1 Cor. 12:3).

We must remember that the earliest Christians, including Paul, were Jews. They were rooted in the Old Testament and were firm in their belief in one God. It would be difficult for them to ascribe divine dignity to any human being, especially one who died on a cross. But under the leading of the Spirit and a deepening understanding of their experience with the living Lord, they began to use language that acknowledged the deity of Christ. They did not use the technical terms employed by later generations. They used language drawn from the Old Testament and their Jewish background. They never compromised their belief in Jesus' humanity. But they were led to confess that Jesus is the divine Son of God.

The intercession of Christ.—Basic to the meaning of the ascension is that Jesus is present in heaven in His glorified humanity for us. Some have assumed that when Jesus returned to the Father, He left his humanity on earth. If that were the case, however, the incarnation would have no continuing significance for Him. The role of Jesus as heavenly mediator presupposes His continuing humanity. The implication is that the incarnation is more than a theophany (a temporary manifestation only). The incarnation continues. Jesus reigns as the divine-human Lord.

We must not forget that Jesus appears in heaven *for us*. This emphasis occurs frequently in the Book of Hebrews. Jesus has entered the inner sanctuary "on our behalf" (6:20). He "entered heaven itself, now to appear *for us* in God's presence" (9:24, author's italics). Now "we have confidence to enter the Most Holy Place by the blood of Jesus, by a new and living way opened *for us* through the curtain, that is, his body" (10:19-20, author's italics). As exalted Lord and High Priest, "he is able to have completely those who come to God through him, because he always lives to intercede for them" (7:25).

What is involved in Jesus' intercession for us? We should not think that Jesus pleads with a reluctant Father (Rom. 8:32). Rather the very presence of Jesus in heaven is the guarantee of our acceptance with God. It is a reminder that God is for us and not against us. For this reason, we are invited to "approach the throne of grace with confidence, so that we may receive mercy and find grace to help us in our time of need" (Heb. 4:16).

The bestowal of the Spirit.—As a result of His exaltation, Jesus bestowed the Spirit on His followers. This took place on the Day of Pentecost. Incredible things happened. There was a sound like the blowing of a violent wind, what seemed to be tongues of fire rested on each of them, and they spoke with other tongues (Acts 2:3-4). The gospel was preached. About three thousand people received the message and were baptized (Acts 2:41). Peter put the occasion in perspective. "Exalted to the right hand of God, he has received from the Father the promised Holy Spirit and has poured out what you now see and hear" (Acts 2:33).

To appreciate the story of Pentecost, we must see it in historical and theological perspective. It is an event with several facets of meaning. Among them are the following:

(1) Pentecost is a significant part of God's saving activity. It is a part of the same salvation history which includes the call of Abraham, the Exodus, the incarnation, the cross, and the resurrection. As such, it is unique and unrepeatable.

(2) Pentecost marks the beginning of the church as the body of Christ bearing witness to Him in the world. Some scholars have spoken of Pentecost as the birthday of the church. This does not mean that the church has no antecedents. It has roots in Jesus' calling twelve disciples to be the nucleus of a new Israel and, perhaps, in the Old Testament concept of a faithful remnant.

But in the New Testament sense, the church is grounded in the saving activity of Christ. It is the community of the risen Lord. On the Day of Pentecost, this body of people was unified and empowered to witness.

(3) Pentecost has implications for eschatology and missions. In his sermon, Peter quoted Joel 2:28-32. The passage begins, " 'In the last days,' God says, 'I will pour out my Spirit on all people' " (Acts 2:17). "The last days" is a reference to the messianic era, the time before the end. The "last days" began with the incarnation and will end with the consummation. They are the days in which the age to come overlaps the present age. The gift of the Spirit is a foretaste of the future in the present.

The phrase "upon all people" points to the universal scope of the Spirit's activity. In the present context, it anticipates the mission to the

Gentiles. Just before Pentecost, Jesus told His disciples, "You will be my witnesses in Jerusalem, and in all Judea and Samaria, and to the ends of the earth" (Acts 1:8). These words reinforce the Great Commission, "Therefore go and *make disciples of all nations,* baptizing them in the name of the Father and of the Son and of the Holy Spirit, and teaching them to obey everything I have commanded you. And surely I will be with you always, to the very end of the age" (Matt. 28:19-20, author's italics).

(4) Pentecost is the reversal of Babel. The story of Babel (Gen. 11:1-9) represents God's judgment on human pride (compare ch. 1). His judgment took the form of a confusion of language so that the people could not understand one another. The confusion of language is an appropriate symbol for the barriers of misunderstanding and hostility which exist between people.

But this judgment was reversed at Pentecost. God's saving activity was proclaimed with no language impediment. People from different nations exclaimed, "Are not all these men who are speaking Galileans? Then how is it that each of us hears them in his own native language?" (Acts 2:7-8). The "tongues" (*glossolalia*) of Acts 2, therefore, refer to the intelligible proclamation of the gospel. The whole scene underlines the universality of the message of salvation as well as the mission of the people of God.

Notes

1. A. W. W. Dale, *The Life of R. W. Dale of Birmingham* (London: Hodder and Stoughton, 1898), pp. 642-643.

2. F. F. Bruce, *The Gospel of John* (Grand Rapids: William B. Eerdmans Publishing Co., 1983), pp. 369-379.

3. There is a possible exception in John 20:8. Cf. Bruce, *The Gospel of John,* pp. 387-88.

4. Walter Kunneth, *The Theology of the Resurrection,* p. 97.

5. James Denney, *The Way Everlasting* (London: Hodder and Stoughton, 1911), p. 188.

6. On the relation of Acts 1:9-11 to the ascension scene in Luke 24:50-53 see Ray Summers, *Commentary on Luke* (Waco: Word Books, Publisher,

1972), pp. 336-338 and Murray J. Harris, *Raised Immortal; Resurrection and Immortality in the New Testament*, pp. 86-88.

7. Behind the expression "the right hand of God" stands Psalm 110:1. The New Testament quotes this passage more than any other one from the Old Testament. See D. M. Hay, *Glory at the Right Hand: Psalm 110 in Early Christianity* (New York: Abingdon Press, 1973).

8. See the discussion in Guthrie, *Christian Doctrine*, pp. 270-282.

Bibliography

Beasley-Murray, G. R. *Christ is Alive!* London: Lutterworth Press, 1947.

Conner, W. T. *The Resurrection of Christ*. Nashville: The Sunday School Board of the Southern Baptist Convention, 1926.

Davies, J. G. *He Ascended in to Heaven*. London: Lutterworth Press, 1958.

Donne, Brian K. *Christ Ascended*. Exeter: The Paternoster Press, 1983.

Harris, Murray J. *Raised Immortal; Resurrection and Immortality in the New Testament*. Grand Rapids: William B. Eerdmans Publishing Co., 1983.

Holwerda, David E. "Ascension." *The International Standard Bible Encyclopedia*. Revised. Ed. by Geoffrey Bromiley. Grand Rapids: William B. Eerdmans Publishing Co., 1979. Vol. I, pp. 310-313.

Jansen, John Frederick. *The Resurrection of Jesus Christ in New Testament Theology*. Philadelphia: The Westminster Press, 1980.

Kesich, Veselin. *The First Day of the New Creation*. Crestwood, New York: St. Vladimir's Seminary Press, 1982.

Kunneth, Walter. *The Theology of the Resurrection*. St. Louis: Concordia Publishing House, 1951.

Ladd, George Eldon. *I Believe in the Resurrection of Jesus*. Grand Rapids: William B. Eerdmans Publishing Co., 1975.

Ramsey, A. Michael. *The Resurrection of Christ*. Philadelphia: The Westminster Press, 1946.

Tenney, Merrill C. *The Reality of the Resurrection*. New York: Harper & Row, 1963.

Toon, Peter. *The Ascension of Our Lord*. Nashville: Thomas Nelson Publishers, 1984.

Torrance, Thomas F. *Space, Time and Resurrection*. Grand Rapids: William B. Eerdmans Publishing Co., 1976.

6

Perspectives on Salvation

The chorus of a popular hymn of salvation speaks of being

> Saved by his pow'r divine,
> Saved to new life sublime!
> Life now is sweet and my joy is complete,
> For I'm saved, saved, saved![1]

In the last three chapters, we have considered God's provision of salvation in the life, death, and resurrection of Christ. In this chapter, several related questions must be considered: What is the nature of salvation which God has provided? How do you get salvation? What are some ways salvation is described in the New Testament?

The Basic Elements

A good place to begin in answering these questions is Ephesians 2:8-10. This passage is Paul's "gospel in a nutshell." It is a concise summary of his understanding of salvation.

> For it is by *grace* you have been *saved,* through *faith*—and this not from yourselves, it is the gift of God—not by works, so that no one can boast. For we are God's workmanship, created in Christ Jesus to do good *works*, which God prepared in advance for us to do (author's italics).

The thought of these verses centers around four interrelated themes: salvation, grace, faith, and works.

Salvation

The meaning of salvation.—The word *salvation* means rescue or deliverance. In the broadest sense, salvation implies deliverance from

118

any threatening situation. Illustrations of this meaning are found in numerous daily crises.

Several years ago a plane crashed into a river on takeoff. Numerous lives were lost. A flight attendant managed to escape from the plane through a forward exit. Shaken by the impact of the crash and stunned by the icy river, she was unable to reach the shore. A passerby noted her peril. Risking his life, he plunged into the river and pulled her to safety. He *saved* her life.

A large hotel was engulfed in flames. An elderly lady was trapped in her room on the third floor. A fireman climbed the ladder and entered the smoke-filled room. He held the lady firmly in his arms as he climbed down the ladder to safety. Her life was *saved*.

This understanding corresponds to the biblical usage. When Israel was enslaved in Egypt God *saved* them from bondage. A typical testimony is, "Blessed are you, O Israel! Who is like you, a people *saved* by the Lord?" (Deut. 33:29, author's italics). When the disciples were threatened in the Galilean storm, they cried, "Lord, save us! We're going to drown!" (Matt. 8:25).

Each of these illustrations speaks of salvation from physical peril. The most profound meaning of salvation, however, is deliverance from the lostness caused by sin. When used in this sense, the term is enriched and expanded.

First, *salvation* becomes a comprehensive word which sums up all the blessings resulting from God's saving activity in Christ. This is the meaning of salvation in such expressions as, "By this gospel you are saved" (1 Cor. 15:2), "the gospel of your salvation" (Eph. 1:13), "the grace of God that brings salvation" (Titus 2:11), "such a great salvation" (Heb. 2:3) and "the salvation we share" (Jude 3).

In the Old Testament, God wrought many deliverances. But none of them compare with what He provided in Christ. All that preceded Christ was partial and preliminary. In Christ alone has God provided the ultimate salvation. This salvation exceeds even the Exodus from Egypt. That event was a promise of a greater deliverance which was realized in Christ. As the fulfillment of God's promised blessings, Christ is "the source of eternal salvation for all who obey him" (Heb. 5:9).

Second, it involves a new dimension of life. Salvation is no mere escapism. We are saved not only *from* a deadly peril but also *to* a new way of living. Notice the different ways this is expressed. We are delivered from condemnation to eternal life (John 3:16-17), from slavery to freedom (Gal. 5:1), from guilt to forgiveness (Eph. 1:7), from being aliens to being citizens (Eph. 2:12-13; 1 Pet. 1:10), from fear of evil powers to victory and assurance (1 John 4:18; 2 Tim. 1:7), from darkness to light (1 Pet. 2:9).

The tenses of salvation.—Salvation occurs in three tenses—past, present, and future.[2]

(1) As a past event, salvation refers (a) to the provision of salvation in the life, death, and resurrection of Jesus and (b) to the time when we, by faith, accepted salvation as our own (compare Eph. 2:8; Titus 3:5; 2 Tim. 1:9).

The second reference focuses on becoming a Christian. It reminds us of the time we accepted God's gift of salvation. Confronted by the gospel, we yielded our lives to Jesus as Savior and entered the Christian way of life. The beginning of the Christian life is often called *conversion*. *Conversion* denotes the act of turning around, a change of direction. It is related in meaning to *repentance* which means a change of mind leading to a change of life. When we first experience salvation, therefore, our lives are reoriented. We are rescued from lostness, and we enter a new relationship with God through Christ.

It is possible to speak of a common content in conversion—grace, faith, peace, joy. But we should not expect every conversion experience to take the same form. Conversion experiences are as diverse as the individuals themselves. We should be especially careful not to make the shape of our own experience normative for every other person. Sometimes this can lead to the mistaken notion that God must work in exactly the same way in every life. Careful attention to the testimonies of other people reveals a rich variety in patterns of experience.[3]

Sometimes conversion occurs in a dramatic way. Paul, for example, was converted in a blinding experience on the Damascus road (Acts 9:3-19; 22:6-16; 26:12-18). The change was sudden and unexpected. From a zealous persecutor of the church (Acts 9:12), Paul became an equally avid missionary for Christ (Acts 9:22).

Not all conversions, however, occur in such a dramatic way. In Acts 16:11-15 we are told how Lydia became a Christian. In contrast to Paul, Lydia's conversion was quiet and unspectacular. "The Lord opened her heart to respond to Paul's message" (v. 14). Though less dramatic, her experience was just as real and meaningful.

God may work in different ways in each of our lives. He always treats us as individuals. Numerous factors enter into the shape of our experience—age, psychological profile, religious environment (or lack of it), and culture. God works through these elements, but they cannot provide a complete explanation of the change that occurs in becoming a Christian. Conversion is ultimately God's work.

(2) Salvation is also a present experience (1 Cor. 1:18; 2 Cor. 2:15). As a present experience, salvation involves a process of growth. Conversion is not the end of God's way with us. It is only a beginning. Another way of saying this is, "If by God's grace I'm not what I was, by God's grace I'm not all that I will be." God sustains us in the Christian life. He also continues to work in us to accomplish His purpose.

New Christians are aptly described as babes in Christ. Once birth has taken place, however, there is need for growth. Peter urged, "Like newborn babies, crave pure spiritual milk, so that by it you may grow up in your salvation, now that you have tasted that the Lord is good" (1 Pet. 2:2).

The emergence of life can be an exciting experience. It is the occasion for joy and gratitude. But if growth does not follow birth, excitement gives way to disappointment. Physical and intellectual growth is expected. Such growth is necessary to meet the strenuous challenges which life brings. This is true spiritually as well. If we do not mature in the experience of salvation, we will never reach our potential for Christ. We will always be hindered by spiritual ineffectiveness and will forfeit much of the joy of mature Christian living (compare 1 Cor. 3:1-3; Heb. 5:11-14).

But do we ever completely grow up? Do we ever reach a plateau which signals that we have it made? Or is spiritual growth a lifelong process? The answer to such questions depends on the standard of maturity by which we measure ourselves. Does the New Testament provide us with such a standard? Yes! Paul spoke of "mature manhood, measured by nothing less than the full stature of Christ" (Eph. 4:13, NEB). To know the real extent of our growth, we must measure ourselves by Him. To measure ourselves by Him is to realize how far short we fall.

Growing in grace, therefore, is a process that lasts throughout life. We are never done with it. We may be more mature than when we began, but we still have a lot of growing to do. Sometimes growth involves struggle. Rarely, if ever, is maturity achieved without pain. The "full stature of Christ" is not reached overnight. There are no magical formulas or shortcuts. Maturity can only be approximated by a lifetime of devotion and service.

Such considerations should provide a constant encouragement for us to "grow up into him who is the Head, that is, Christ" (Eph. 4:15). Salvation is a continuous adventure, and it is never boring. There are always new depths to fathom, new heights to scale and new challanges to face. In this process we should realize that we are not left to strive toward maturity by our resources alone. God continues to work in us to help us to grow. "It is God who works in you to will and to act according to his good purpose" (Phil. 2:13).

A realistic model for Christian growth is provided by Paul. To the Philippians he wrote:

> Not that I claim to have achieved all this, nor to have reached perfection already. But I keep going on, trying to grasp that purpose for which Christ Jesus grasped me. My brothers, I do not consider myself to have grasped it fully even now. But I do concentrate on this: I forget all that lies behind me and with hands outstretched to whatever lies ahead I go straight for the goal—my reward the honour of my high calling by God in Christ Jesus" (3:12-14, Phillips).

(3) As a future hope, salvation anticipates the consummation of God's redeeming activity. There is a strong emphasis in the New Testament on this future dimension of salvation. In Romans 13:11, we read that "our salvation is nearer now than when we first believed" (compare 5:9; 8:23; 1 Thess. 5:8-9). Peter affirmed that Christians "through faith are shielded by God's power until the coming of the

salvation to be revealed in the last time" (1 Pet. 1:5; compare 1:9). The author of Hebrews asserted, "So Christ was sacrificed once to take away the sin of many people, and he will appear a second time, not to bear sin, but to bring salvation to those who are waiting for him" (Heb. 9:28). This forward look assumes salvation as a past experience and a present condition. But it points forward to the time when salvation is brought to its fullness.

The emphasis on the future dimension of salvation implies that our present Christian experience, though genuine, is only partial. There is more to come (Rom. 8:18-25; 1 Cor. 2:9). The final defeat of sin, death, and opposition to God will occur in the future. In the meanwhile, we live in the confident expectation that God will complete what He started.

Hope in the consummation of God's saving work involves a threefold assurance. First, hope is grounded in what God has already accomplished in the life, death, and resurrection of Christ. The first coming of Christ was decisive for all of God's future activity.

Second, hope is based on the character of God as faithful. He always keeps His promise. He kept His promise to Abraham. God was unfailing in His covenant relation with Israel. He will also fulfill the promises He has made with us in Christ. We can be confident, therefore, "that he who began a good work in you will carry it on to completion until the day of Christ Jesus" (Phil. 1:6; compare 1 Cor. 1:9; 2 Cor. 1:18; 1 Thess. 5:24; 2 Thess. 3:3). It is God's faithfulness that ultimately guarantees the fulfillment of His saving work.

Third, hope is authenticated by the Holy Spirit. There are three metaphors in the New Testament which describe the function of the Spirit in relation to the future of salvation. For example, the Spirit is God's *seal* on the life of the believer (2 Cor. 1:21-22; Eph. 1:13). In the ancient world, seals were used to designate possession by an owner. Cattle were branded and slaves were tattooed with the mark of their master. In a similar way, Christians receive the Spirit as a sign of divine ownership. Such a sign is the basis for Christian assurance for the present and the future (2 Tim. 2:19).

The Spirit is also the *guarantee* of the believer's future inheritance (2 Cor. 1:21-22; Eph. 1:13-14). The word *guarantee* is a commercial term. It designates a down payment or first installment. It is money given as a promise that the full amount will be paid in due time. The gift of the Spirit is God's promise that the believer will eventually participate in the fullness of his inheritance. But the Spirit is more than just a promise. In giving the Spirit, God is not just promising the future but actually giving a foretaste of it.

Further, the Spirit is the *firstfruits*. The word *firstfruits* is an agricultural metaphor denoting the first part of the harvest considered as a pledge of the full harvest to come. The meaning is the same as in the case of "seal" and "guarantee." The Spirit is God's pledge that His saving purpose will be consummated.

Grace

The meaning of grace.—Grace is the free, spontaneous, and unmerited love of God for sinful people. It is the divine love experienced as a gift. As such, grace lies at the very heart of the Christian gospel.

In the New Testament, Paul spoke most frequently of grace. Approximately one hundred and one times the word *grace* appears in Paul's letters. He made it clear that divine grace manifested in the person and work of Christ is the basis of salvation. This emphasis is clear in several key references. "All have sinned and fall short of the glory of God, and are justified freely by his grace as a gift through the redemption that came by Christ Jesus" (Rom. 3:23-24). "For if the many died by the trespass of the one man, how much more did God's grace and the gift that came by the grace of the one man, Jesus Christ, overflow to the many!" (Rom. 5:15). "For it is by grace you have been saved" (Eph. 2:8). "For the grace of God that brings salvation has appeared to all men" (Titus 2:11). "He saved us . . . so that having been justified by his grace, we might become heirs having the hope of eternal life" (Titus 3:5-7).

Grace is personal.—God's grace should be understood in personal terms. It is neither an impersonal force nor a spiritual substance which can be dispensed like a prescription by a physician. Grace is not a "thing" which can be detached from God and experienced separately. The grace of God is nothing less than God Himself in His graciousness toward us. Robert McAfee Brown has written, "Grace is not something God himself gives us, it is the way he gives us himself."[4] The Gift and the Giver are one. When we experience grace, therefore, we experience God as a gracious personal presence working in our lives.

Grace is free.—To speak of grace as free means that it is unmerited. Divine grace and human merit are opposites which cannot co-exist. Grace is always a gift; it is not a reward for services rendered. This means that salvation can never be earned. It can only be accepted. If we could achieve salvation, we might have a basis for boasting (Eph. 2:9). But such pride is sinful. Thus, if salvation could be achieved by good works, it would involve us more deeply in the sin from which we need to be delivered! The message is clear: "But when the kindness and love of God our Savior appeared, he saved us, not because of righteous things we had done, but because of his mercy" (Titus 3:4-5). This truth is beautifully expressed in the following words:

> Great God of wonders! all thy ways
>   Display the attributes divine;
> But countless acts of pardoning grace
>   Beyond thine other wonders shine:
> Who is pardoning God like Thee?
> Or who has grace so rich and free?
> In wonder lost, with trembling joy,
>   We take the pardon of our God:
> Pardon for crimes of deepest dye.
>   A pardon bought with Jesus' blood:
> Who is a pardoning God like Thee?
> Or who has grace so rich and free?
> O may this strange, this matchless grace,
>   This God-like miracle of love,
> Fill the wide earth with grateful praise,
>   As now it fills the choirs above!
> Who is a pardoning God like Thee?
> Or who has grace so rich and free?[5]

Faith

Faith is the means by which we receive God's gift of salvation. It involves an attitude of openness and receptivity to the saving presence of God in Christ. Faith is a genuine human response, but it is evoked or drawn forth by God's gracious activity. For this reason, faith should not be thought of as a work which deserves a reward. In grace God in Christ gives Himself to us; in faith we give ourselves to Him. This response involves both knowledge and trust.

Faith as knowledge.—A popular misconception of faith is that it is believing what cannot be proved. This leaves the impression that faith is contrary to and a substitute for reason. It is true that there is a dimension of a genuine mystery in the Christian faith. The great events of salvation history (for example, the incarnation and resurrection) cannot be reduced to a simple rational formula (compare 1 Tim. 3:16). This does not mean, however, that they are irrational. Faith may occasionally outrun reason, but it does not outrage reason.

Faith is believing based on knowledge. It is not an emotional experience that dispenses with the intellect. Knowledge keeps faith from becoming a blind leap into the dark.

The New Testament emphasizes the necessity of knowing certain things and *believing that* they are true. Consider the following examples. "If you confess with your mouth, 'Jesus is Lord,' and believe in your heart *that* God raised him from the dead, you will be saved" (Rom. 10:9-10, author's italics). "And without faith it is impossible to please God, because anyone who comes to him must *believe that* he exists and *that* he rewards those who seek him" (Heb. 11:6, author's italics). "This is how you can recognize the Spirit of God: Every spirit that *acknowledges that* Jesus Christ has come in the flesh is from God" (1 John 4:2-3, author's italics). "Everyone who *believes that* Jesus is the Christ is born of God" (1 John 5:1, author's italics).

The significance of knowledge can also be seen by looking at the content of the earliest Christian preaching. Sample sermons by Peter and Paul are found in Acts 2—5; 10; and 13. The basic themes of these sermons are as follows:

(1) God has begun to fulfill His promises (Acts 2:16; 3:18, 24; 10:43; 13:32-33).

(2) The new age of God's reign has dawned (Acts 2:17 *ff.*; 10:38; 13:38-39).

(3) This is the result of the coming of Jesus into the world. There is

a strong emphasis on Jesus' life, death, and resurrection as the focal point of God's saving activity (Acts 2:22-24; 3:15; 4:10; 10:38-40; 13:30).

(4) The risen Christ is Lord of the church (Acts 2:33,36; 4:11; 10:36).

(5) The risen Lord will return to complete God's saving work (Acts 3:20; 10:42).

On the basis of this message, there was a call to repent and believe in Christ as the Savior and Lord (Acts 2:38-41; 3:19; 10:43; 13:38-39). Thus, faith in the New Testament is never a vague "belief in belief." It has a definite content, namely, the saving work of God in Christ. Faith assumes knowledge of and assent to these basic facts.

But mental assent alone is never a sufficient response to the gospel. James reminded us that "even the demons believe" (2:19), but they do not cease their demonic activity. We can affirm the existence of God and know the facts about Christ and, yet, not make a positive response. There is more to faith than "believing that . . ."

Faith as trust.—Faith is primarily trust. The word *trust* is most meaningful in the context of personal relationships. When we speak of trusting "things," the term is used in a secondary sense. Trust is basically something we have in other people. It involves a commitment to persons in relationships of mutual self-giving. To trust God, therefore, is to commit oneself to a personal relationship with Him. A relationship of trust involves knowledge of God, but also means a willingness to put ourselves completely in God's hands.

Faith as trust is expressed in the New Testament by the phrase "believe in." For example, "To all who received him, to those who believed in his name, he gave the right to become children of God" (John 1:12). "Whoever believes in him shall not perish but have eternal life" (John 3:16). "Whoever believes in him is not condemned" (v. 18). "But also for us, to whom God will credit righteousness—for us who believe in him who raised Jesus our Lord from the dead" (Rom. 4:24). Paul responded to the jailer's question, "What must I do to be saved?" with, "Believe in the Lord Jesus, and you will be saved" (Acts 16:31). "Believing in" Jesus involves the response of the whole person to Christ as Savior.

The nature of saving faith has been aptly expressed by Martin Luther:

> There are two kinds of believing: First a believing about God which means that I believe in what is said of God is true. This faith is rather a form of knowledge than a faith—Men possessing it can say, repeating what others have said: I believe that there is a God. I believe that Christ was born, died, rose again for me. But what the real faith is and how powerful a thing it is, of this they know nothing. . . . There is secondly, a believing in God which means that I put my trust in Him, give myself up to thinking that I can have dealings with Him, and believe without any doubt that He will be and do to me according to the things said of Him. Such faith which throws itself upon God, whether in life or in death, alone makes a Christian man.[6]

Works

Salvation produces a change of direction and character in a person's life. To be saved, therefore, implies that one will live in obedience to the will of God. Salvation and discipleship should never be separated. This is underlined by the strong emphasis on good works in the New Testament.

Works: the purpose of salvation.—The purpose of salvation is a life of devoted service. This is made clear in Ephesians 2:10. "For we are God's workmanship, created in Christ Jesus to do good works, which God prepared in advance for us to do." That we are "God's workmanship" means that it is He who has made us Christians. The origin of salvation in grace is thereby reaffirmed (compare 1 Cor. 5:10). "Created in Christ Jesus" is not a reference to natural birth but to the new creation (compare 2 Cor. 5:17). The purpose of God's saving (re-creating) work is expressed in the phrase "for good works." God does not intend for us to bask in inward experiences, but to live lives that reflect our relationship with Him. Good works, therefore, are not incidental to salvation. They are part of God's eternal purpose for us.

It is essential, however, to keep the proper relationship between salvation and works. Works are never the root of salvation. Salvation is always and only by grace through faith. But works are the fruit of salvation. If we are not saved *by* works, we are saved *for* them. Paul stressed that Jesus "gave himself to redeem us from all wickedness and to purify for himself a people that are his very own, eager to do what is good" (Titus 2:14). Paul's prayer for Christians was that they might live "a life worthy of the Lord and may please him in every way: bearing fruit in every good work, growing in the knowledge of God" (Col. 1:10).

Works: the evidence of faith.—A strong emphasis on works as the evidence of vital faith is found in James 2:14-26. Two related questions express James's concern: "What good is it, my brothers, if a man claims to have faith but has no deeds? Can such faith save him?" (v. 14). Two related statements provide an answer. "Faith by itself, if it is not accompanied by action, is dead" (v. 17). "A person is justified by what he does and not by faith alone" (v. 24).

The teaching of James on faith and works has often caused controversy among Christians. He has been accused of contradicting Paul's emphasis on justification by faith alone (compare especially Rom. 4). Martin Luther found the epistle so objectionable at this point that he regarded it as "an epistle of straw." He is not the only person to find James uncongenial. Such a conclusion, however, is unfortunate. Close attention to these passages shows that the two apostles complement rather than contradict one another.[7] The following considerations will help to clarify this point.

(1) Paul and James were addressing different issues. Paul was speaking to the problem of legalism. He was concerned with those who believed they could make themselves acceptable to God by their deeds. James, on the other hand, was addressing people whose lives gave no evidence that they possessed what they professed.

(2) They were asking different, but related, questions. Paul was asking, "How can a person be brought into a right relationship with God?" His answer was, "By a declaration of acquittal called justification." James was asking, "What difference does justification make in the way a person lives?" His answer was, "It leads to a life of loving service."

(3) Both apostles used the word *faith*. Paul understood faith to be the commitment of oneself to God in a relationship of trust. James was critical of a false view of faith. It was a view that limited faith to

knowledge and assent (v. 19). Correct opinions are important, but they are not enough. One's life must be brought under the control of Christ.

(4) Similarly, both apostles referred to "works." When Paul argued that we are not saved by works, he meant legalistic deeds performed to secure God's favor (Rom. 4:2-4; compare Gal. 2:16). When James urged the necessity of works, he meant deeds of love which are the fruit of saving faith (2:16-17; compare Paul's emphasis in Gal. 5:6 on "faith expressing itself through love").

(5) Both men illustrated their points from the life of Abraham. For Paul, Abraham was an example of justification by faith (Rom. 4:16-22). Paul quoted Genesis 15:6, where God promised Abraham and his aged wife that they would have a son. Though it seemed humanly impossible, "Abraham believed the Lord, and he credited it to him as righteousness." For James, Abraham was an example of justification by works. He referred to Genesis 22, where Abraham showed his willingness to sacrifice his son at God's command. Such confidence in God demonstrated the depth and genuineness of the patriarch's faith.

Thus, in their emphasis on works, Paul and James reinforced each other. Their words are a warning against preaching that would separate faith and works, salvation and discipleship.

Pictures of Salvation

The New Testament describes the meaning of salvation by using many different metaphors. The writers speak of justification, sanctification, adoption, reconciliation, the restoration of God's image, the new birth, eternal life, and incorporation into Christ. These metaphors do not describe separate events which are experienced in temporal sequence. They are best thought of as pictures of salvation. All these pictures are different ways of representing what God has done for us in His saving activity.

Salvation as Justification

Justification involves a change of status in our relation to God. The background of the term is legal. The scene is a law court in which the defendant stands before the judge. There is no question about the proper verdict. The defendant is guilty. Nor is there any doubt about the sentence. "The wages of sin is death" (Rom. 6:23). But a strange thing happens. Instead of the death penalty, another verdict is announced. It is the verdict of acquittal. Sin is forgiven (Rom. 4:3-8). Guilt is remitted.

This is particularly meaningful when we remember that guilt is one of the consequences of sin. And guilt is more than a mere feeling. It is the status of one who has sinned against God and is liable to punishment (compare ch. 1 on the consequences of sin). But justification changes our status. We are no longer condemned by our sin and guilt. Our new status is nothing less than a right relationship with God who is both Judge and Savior.

At least four elements enter into the meaning of justification in the New Testament.

Justification, the cross, and resurrection.—The ground or basis for God's justifying activity is the death and resurrection of Christ. In relation to the cross, Paul wrote, "A man who has faith is now freely acquitted in the eyes of God by his generous dealing in the redemptive act of Christ Jesus. God has appointed him as the means of propitiation, a propitiation accomplished by the shedding of his blood, to be made effective in ourselves by faith" (Rom. 3:24-25, Phillips). In relation to the resurrection, he spoke of "Jesus our Lord, who was delivered to death for our sins and raised again to secure our justification" (Rom. 4:25, Phillips; compare 5:10; 8:34; 2 Tim. 2:11).

Justification and grace.—The provision of justification is the gift of God's grace. The phrase "justification by grace" is at the heart of Paul's gospel (see Rom. 3:24-25; 4:4,16; Titus 3:7). All thought of earning God's forgiveness is excluded. Our experience of acquittal is undeserved.

Justification and faith.—This gracious provision is received by faith. In Galatians 2:16 we read, "A man is not justified by observing the law, but by faith in Jesus Christ. So we, too, have put our faith in Christ Jesus that we may be justified by faith in Christ and not by observing the law, because by observing the law no one will be justified" (compare Ps. 143:2). It would be difficult to find a more forceful statement of justification by faith. Any appeal of self-righteousness is abolished. There is no other way to experience God's acquittal than commitment to Christ in a relationship of trust.

Justification—present and future.—Justification is both a present experience and a future hope. As a present experience, it stands at the beginning of the Christian life (Rom. 5:1,9; 1 Cor. 6:11; Titus 3:7). Because of this, we do not have to wait in nervous uncertainty for the final verdict. God has already acquitted us.

Nevertheless, there is a future dimension to justification. "But by faith we eagerly await through the Spirit the righteousness for which we hope" (Gal. 5:5). The word translated "righteousness" is the word for *justification*. It expresses the hope for a favorable verdict in the last judgment. For those who trust Christ, such a verdict is assured because of the present experience of justification. The final verdict "not guilty" is realized in our present experience. Such a hope, therefore, is not "hoping against hope." It is a steadfast hope which is fostered and kept alive by the Holy Spirit (compare Eph. 1:13-14).

Salvation as Sanctification

Sanctification involves being set apart to God and gradually transformed into His likeness. It describes the beginning of the Christian life (set apart) and the development of that life (gradually transformed). Thus, sanctification is both an act and a process.

The background of this metaphor is the Old Testament concept of holiness. The word *holy* means "to be separate" or "to be set apart." With reference to God, it means that He is transcendent. He is before and above everything creaturely. Holiness is God's basic nature that separates Him from everything that is not God. A characteristic designation for God is "the Holy One of Israel" (Ps. 89:19; Isa. 1:4; 12:6; 40:25; Jer. 50:29). God's transcendence, however, is not to be understood as remoteness. It is His otherness (Isa. 46:5-9). Though He is "wholly other," He is present with His people (Hos. 11:9).

People, places, and things are also called holy. Does this imply that they share in God's deity? No! Deity is unique to God alone. They are holy in a derivative sense. People, places, and things are holy by virtue of their relationship to God. They are set apart by God as instruments of His purpose. Israel, for example, is called "a kingdom of priests and a holy nation" (Ex. 19:6). God set this nation apart for a special role in salvation history. Such a relationship always involves responsibility. God's Word to those whom He sets apart is: "I am the Lord your God; consecrate yourselves and be holy, because I am holy" (Lev. 11:44).

There are three considerations which will help us understand the meaning of sanctification (or holiness) in the New Testament.

Sanctification as a divine work.—Sanctification is God's work. God separates us from evil and works to transform us into the divine image. Sometimes this activity is attributed to the Father. "May God himself, the God of peace, sanctify you through and through" (1 Thess. 5:23). Occasionally it is associated with the Son. Paul spoke of "Christ Jesus, who has become for us wisdom from God— that is, our righteousness, holiness and redemption" (1 Cor. 1:30). Frequently, it is ascribed to the Holy Spirit. "From the beginning God chose you to be saved through the sanctifying work of the Spirit" (2 Thess. 2:13; compare 1 Pet. 1:2). The thrust of these passages is that sanctification is not a human achievement of which we can boast. From beginning to end, it is the work of the Triune God.

Sanctification as a completed work.—From one point of view, sanctification is accomplished fact. The decisive transition has been made. We already belong to God. "But you were washed, you were sanctified, you were justified in the name of the Lord Jesus Christ" (1 Cor. 6:11). The verbs in this verse are in the past tense. They point to a completed act. In other words, the Corinthians had already been acquitted and set apart to serve God.

It is also important to notice that Christians are usually called saints (Acts 9:13; Rom. 1:7; 16:15; 2 Cor. 1:1; 13:13; Heb. 6:10; Rev. 11:18). This name is not reserved for an elite group within the church. It refers to all Christians. Thus, sanctification stands at the beginning of the Christian life. It is not an optional or extra feature of that life. To be a Christian is to be sanctified.

Sanctification as a continuing work.—From another point of view, sanctification is a process. As a process, it involves growing "in the grace and knowledge of our Lord Jesus Christ" (2 Pet. 3:18). Though we already belong to God, we gradually become more and more what He wants us to be. Daily we experience more fully what it means to be set apart for Him.

Growth in sanctification does not mean that we are passive in the process. Though it is God's work, it is also our responsibility. Discipline and effort are required (compare Phil. 2:12-13). This explains the many ethical exhortations in the New Testament. So, the Corinthians are encouraged to purify themselves "perfecting holiness out of reverence for God" (2 Cor. 7:1). The Thessalonians are told to avoid sexual immorality because God wants them to be holy (1 Thess. 4:3). Timothy was instructed that the person who cleanses himself "will be an instrument for noble purposes, made holy, useful for the Master and prepared to do any good work" (2 Tim. 2:21). Such passages remind us that the Christian life is a journey which involves striving. Progress is not always easy, but it is possible because of the indwelling and empowering of the Spirit.

Salvation as Adoption

Adoption is the act by which a child not born into a family becomes a member of the family and an heir. The word translated *adoption* occurs five times in the New Testament. All these are found in Paul's letters (Rom. 8:15,23; 9:4; Gal. 4:5; Eph. 1:5). He used the metaphor to portray a present experience and a future hope.

Adoption as a present experience.—This aspect of adoption is explained by the following statement:

> For you have not received a spirit of slavery leading to fear again, but you have received a spirit of adoption as sons by which we cry out "Abba! Father!" The Spirit Himself bears witness with our spirit that we are the children of God, and if children, heirs also, heirs of God and fellow heirs with Christ (Rom. 8:15-17, NASB; compare Gal. 4:4-7).

The emphasis is not that everyone is a child of God by virtue of creation. Rather those are His children who receive His salvation.

As children of God's family, we have a unique privilege. We are able to address God as Father. The word "Abba" is an Aramaic term. It is a term of affection. A Jewish child used this word in addressing his earthly father. Pious Jews avoided the term in speaking to God for fear of over-familiarity. Yet this is the word Jesus used in His prayer in Gethsemane (Mark 14:36). Many scholars believe that the first Christians addressed God in this way because Jesus taught them to do so. Without compromising God's majesty, the word "Abba" speaks of the warm, intimate fellowship which grace makes possible.

As children of God we also have a unique assurance. Confidence that we belong to God is not grounded in ourselves. The basis of assurance is the Spirit of God. Phillips' translation of Romans 8:16 makes this clear. "The Spirit himself endorses our inward conviction that we really are the children of God." This is a more dependable foundation than the state of our emotions in any given moment.

Adoption as a future hope.—This feature of adoption is stated in Romans 8:23-24: "We ourselves, who have the firstfruits of the Spirit, groan inwardly as we wait eagerly for our adoption as sons, the redemption of our bodies. For in this hope we were saved." In one sense, we have already been adopted. In another sense, we are still waiting for it. The future dimension of adoption involves the redemption of the body (that is, its deliverance from weakness, decay, and death). This hope, which is inherent in the meaning of salvation, is sustained by the presence of God's Spirit.

Salvation as the Restoration of God's Image

God's purpose in salvation is to restore His image in us. This is particularly important when we remember that the image of God is essential to what it means to be human (Gen. 1:26-27). Though the image is still present in us, it has been marred by our sinfulness (compare ch. 1 on the meaning of the image and the effects of sin). When we become Christians, a restoration process begins. This process is carried on throughout life and is completed when Christ returns.

There are several references in the New Testament to this way of understanding salvation. In Romans 8:29 we read that God predestined us "to be conformed to the likeness of his Son." The only true model of what it means to be in God's image is Christ. He is not only the revelation of God's nature but also the revelation of God's intention for humanity. Only by becoming like Jesus Christ, therefore, can we realize God's purpose for us.

Paul reminded the Colossians that this transformation had already begun. "You have taken off your old self with its practices, and have put on the new self, which is being renewed in knowledge in the image of its Creator" (Col. 3:9-10; compare Eph. 4:24). He made the same point to the Corinthians. We "are being transformed into his likeness with ever-increasing glory, which comes from the Lord, who is the Spirit" (2 Cor. 3:18). Through this transformation, we begin to realize what it means to be created in God's image. This is something that cannot be adequately grasped apart from salvation.

The fullness of the image belongs to the future. John wrote: "Dear friends, now are we children of God, and what we will be has not yet been made known. But we know that when he appears, we shall be like him, for we shall see him as he is. Everyone who has this hope in him purifies himself, just as he is pure" (1 John 3:2-3). From this passage, several truths should be considered.

1. There is the contrast between "now" and "not yet." This underlines the emphasis on salvation as a present experience and a future hope which characterizes the whole New Testament.

2. There is the contrast between the known and the unknown. We know something of the future because of our present experience. But we do not know all that is involved in the final transformation. We still walk by faith (compare 1 Cor. 13:12).

3. The future transformation is associated with the second coming of Christ.

4. Being like Christ does not mean that we will be divine. We are creatures dependent on God now and forever. Fulfillment of the divine image in us refers to the perfection of our humanity.

5. This hope has implications for the way we live in the present (v. 3; compare Matt. 5:8).

Salvation as Reconciliation

Reconciliation means the restoration of fellowship between people who have been estranged. It involves a change of relationship from enmity to friendship and from conflict to peace. There are two dimensions to reconciliation: the vertical and the horizontal.

The vertical: man reconciled to God.—The New Testament does not speak of God being reconciled to man. God is the subject of the verb "reconcile." Man is the object. The emphasis is that man is reconciled to God. This underscores two basic truths.

First, our sin has created the barrier between us and God. God has not arbitrarily withheld His blessings from us. The alienation is our fault. So serious is the breach that we are called "enemies" of God (Rom. 5:10; Col. 1:21; Jas. 4:4). It is impossible to repair the relationship from our side. Strive as we may, we cannot overcome the barrier of our own sin.

Second, God has taken the initiative to reconcile us to Himself (2 Cor. 5:18-19). The One against whom we have sinned has acted to do away with sin. Healing has come from the One whom we have wounded. Thus reconciliation is both God's accomplishment and His gift. This is how Paul explained it:

> For if, when we were God's enemies, we were reconciled to him through the death of his Son, how much more, having been reconciled, shall we be saved through his life! Not only is this so, but we also rejoice in God through our Lord Jesus Christ, through whom we have now received reconciliation (Rom. 5:10-11).

The horizontal: reconciliation with other people.—The reconciliation we receive from God requires that we be reconciled with one another. This involves breaking down walls that divide people and make fellowship impossible. An illustration of such division today is the Berlin wall. This structure symbolizes a world torn by strife, hatred, and misunderstanding. Jesus died to abolish such barriers among people.

The horizontal dimension of reconciliation is asserted in Ephesians 2:13-16. The heart of this passage is verse 14: "For he himself is our peace, who has made the two one and has destroyed the barrier, the dividing wall of hostility." The "dividing wall" may be an illusion to the wall between the outer and inner courts in the Jerusalem Temple which kept Gentiles and Jews segregated. At places along the wall were signs forbidding Gentiles to go beyond it on pain of death. Such a wall embodied the hostility that separated Jews from Gentiles.

In Christ there is no place for such walls. Christ's death was to create a new humanity in which race, color, economic class, and social standing are no longer decisive. "There is neither Jew nor Greek, slave nor free, male nor female, for you are all one in Christ Jesus" (Gal. 3:28). This does not mean that all distinctions are erased. It means that as barriers to fellowship they have no place in the Christian community. Those who belong to Christ constitute "one person in Christ Jesus" (NEB). Thus we dare not perpetuate the divisions Christ died to destroy.

Salvation as a New Birth

The picture of a new birth is one of the most dramatic in the New Testament. It is a vivid way of emphasizing the life-changing nature of salvation. Like adoption, this metaphor emphasizes that Christians are the redeemed children of God.

Numerous references to the birth metaphor occur in the New Testament, especially in John's writings. The following statement is characteristic of his emphasis: "To all who received him, to those who believed in his name, he gave the right to become children of God—children born not of natural descent, nor of human decision or a husband's will, but born of God" (John 1:12-13; compare 3:1-12; 1 John 2:29; 3:9; 4:7; 5:1,4,18). Peter wrote, "In his great mercy he has given us new birth into a living hope through the resurrection of Jesus Christ from the dead" (1 Pet. 1:3). Similarly, Paul affirmed, "He saved us through the washing of rebirth and renewal by the Holy Spirit" (Titus 3:5).

This same truth is expressed in other ways. It is found in the image of the "new self" (Eph. 4:24), the "new creation" (2 Cor. 5:17; Gal. 6:15) and being made alive (Eph. 2:5). The emphasis is that we were once alive to sin and dead to God but are now alive to God and dead to sin (compare Rom. 6:1-6).

New Testament teaching on the new birth focuses on three points.

Its necessity.—The new birth is a prerequisite for entry into God's kingdom (John 3:3). This necessity grows out of our sinful condition. Efforts at moral reform are commendable but insufficient. When the water is poisoned in the well, it is not enough to whitewash the pump. The change that is needed in human life can only be wrought by the Spirit of God working in our hearts.

Its mystery.—"How can this be?" (John 3:9) is a typical reaction to the mystery of the Spirit's activity. To speak of the new birth as a mystery does not mean that it is irrational or that we should not seek to understand it to the best of our ability. The New Testament neither encourages ignorance nor prohibits inquiry into spiritual matters (2 Tim. 2:15). The mystery of the new birth is a reminder that God's thoughts and ways are always higher than ours (Isa. 55:8-9). The majesty and mystery of God's work can never be exhausted by a rational formula. The new birth is like the wind. We can experience it without knowing everything about it (John 3:8).

Its nature.—The new birth is an inward change brought about by the Spirit of God when we respond in faith to Christ. It does not mean the destruction of our created nature but its reorientation around a different center. Life is no longer centered on self. It is centered on Christ. The nature of this change has been aptly described by W. T. Conner:

> This change is primarily of the nature of a moral and spiritual renewal. It is a change the main significance of which is to be found in the realm of character. In this change the fundamental moral disposition is changed. The affections and activities of life no longer center in self, but in God. Love for God and for one's fellows becomes the controlling factor in life. One dies to sin and rises to walk in newness of life.[8]

Salvation as Eternal Life

New birth leads to new life. This new life is often described by the adjective *eternal*. Like the birth metaphor, the theme of eternal life is found most frequently in the writings of John. In fact, it was John's favorite way of referring to salvation. The purpose of his Gospel is "that you may believe that Jesus is the Christ, the Son of God, and that by believing you may have life in his name" (John 20:31). This, in turn, reflects the reason for Jesus' ministry to the world: "I have come that they may have life, and have it to the full" (John 10:10; compare 3:16-17).

Eternal life: emphasis on quality.—Eternal life should be understood primarily as qualitative rather than quantitative. Endless existence is included, but it is not the major emphasis. Life without end is not a positive hope if it brings continued conflict with sin, guilt, and suffering. It is a positive hope only if the quality of life is transformed into something better. Such a transformation of existence is what Christ accomplished. He has provided the kind of life which people want to experience forever.

Eternal life: life in God's kingdom.—Eternal life comes from another order of existence. It is the life of the kingdom of God (or the life of the coming age) experienced in the present. In John 3 eternal life is said to belong to those who believe in Christ (vv. 15-16). In the same context, the phrases "see the kingdom of God" (v. 3) and "enter the kingdom of God" (v. 5) are used. All three phrases mean the same thing. To enter the kingdom is to have eternal life.

The close relationship between eternal life and the kingdom is illustrated in Mark's Gospel. For example, in Mark 9:43-47 the phrase "to enter life" (vv. 43,45) means the same as "to enter into the kingdom of God" (v. 47). Also, in Mark 10:17-25 "to inherit eternal life" (v. 17), "come, follow me" (v. 21), "to enter the kingdom of God" (v. 23) and "be saved" (v. 26) are used interchangeably. This does not mean that life and kingdom are the same thing. It means that the one who is committed to God's reign has eternal life.

Eternal life: knowledge of God.—One of the most significant statements about eternal life is John 17:3. "Now this is eternal life: that they may know you, the only true God, and Jesus Christ, whom you have sent." *Knowledge* here means knowledge that is enriched by fellowship. It involves knowing as one person knows another person. We know God by committing our lives to Him in a relationship of trust, love, and obedience.

Furthermore, knowledge of God is inseparable from the knowledge of Christ. We know the Father through the Son (John 1:18; 14:8-11). Because of the relationship of Son to the Father, John could say, "God has given us eternal life, and this life is in his Son. He who has the Son has life; he who does not have the Son of God does not have life" (1 John 5:11-12).

Eternal life: present and future.—John's Gospel puts more emphasis on eternal life as a present possession than other New Testament writings. For this reason some scholars have called his view "realized eschatology." This is the belief that the blessings of the future age are already realized in the present. A more accurate description, however, would be "inaugurated eschatology." The blessings of the future have begun to be realized, but their fullness awaits the consummation. Careful reading of John's writings show that his emphasis on the present does not obscure his hope for a future fulfillment (compare John 5:28-29; 6:39,40,44,54; 12:25; 21:22; 1 John 3:2; 4:17).

Salvation as Life in Christ

Eternal life is life "in Christ." This brief phrase is found most often in Paul's writings, though similar expressions also occur in John. Paul used the formula "in Christ" or its equivalents ("in Him" and "in the Lord") approximately two hundred times. It was his favorite way of describing salvation.[9]

Biblical references.—Every aspect of the Christian life is connected to being "in Christ." Numerous references illustrate this point. There is "no condemnation for those who are in Christ Jesus" (Rom. 8:1). "If anyone is in Christ, he is a new creation" (2 Cor. 5:17). God "chose us in him before the creation of the world" (Eph. 1:4). "In him we have redemption through his blood, the forgiveness of sins" (v. 7). "In him and through faith in him we may approach God with freedom and confidence" (Eph. 3:12). In Christ, we are righteous (2 Cor. 5:20-21), sanctified (1 Cor. 1:2) and blessed (Eph. 1:3). Christians not only live in Christ but also die in Him (1 Thess. 4:16) and will be raised in Him (1 Cor. 15:22). Being in Christ brings freedom, peace, joy, purpose, and assurance. It is not difficult to see why the greatest desire of Paul's life was "to gain Christ and be found in him" (Phil. 3:8-9).

Implications.—What does it mean to be "in Christ"? The exact meaning of the phrase is not easy to determine. Different contexts suggest varied nuances. Three proposals deserve attention.

First, "in Christ" pictures the fellowship which the believer has with Christ. As one writer puts it, to be "in Christ" means "the most intimate fellowship imaginable of the Christian with the living spiritual Christ."[10] This is thought to imply that Christ is the environment or atmosphere in which a Christian lives. Just as a fish lives in the water and can live nowhere else, so the Christian's new habitat is Christ.

This view does not mean that we lose our personal identity. We are not absorbed into Christ so that the boundary between Him and us is blurred. The Bible says nothing about losing ourselves in Him. Rather, in Christ we become what we were intended to be. Our uniqueness as individuals is enhanced, not extinguished.

Second, "in Christ" means to be in the church. Life in Christ is a shared life. It involves participation in the church which is the body of Christ (1 Cor. 12:12). The churches in Judea are "in Christ" (Gal. 1:22). All believers are one "in Christ" (Gal. 3:28). Jews and Gentiles share the same promise "in Christ" (Eph. 3:6). Being "in Christ" is, therefore, a corporate experience. Communion with Christ leads to the community of Christ.

Third, "in Christ" means to be in the new phase of salvation history. In Christ's life, death, and resurrection, the new age was inaugurated, a shift from the old age to the new age began. The old age is characterized by sin and death. The new age is one of freedom and life. Though still living in the old age, believers have already experienced the transition from death to life. In Christ the blessings of the new age are present. The phrase "in Christ," therefore, refers to the new historical situation of those who are united by faith with Christ.[11]

Salvation and the Church

Becoming a Christian is an individual affair. When confronted with the gospel, we must decide as individuals whether to accept it or reject it. No one can make the decision for us. We do not experience salvation by proxy.

The New Testament also interprets salvation in a broader context. Salvation is corporate as well as individual. When we become Christians, we become part of a fellowship composed of other Christians. In other words, when we are born again, we do not live in a vacuum. We become part of an already existing family. Conversion, therefore, is the door through which we enter into the community of faith—the church.

Unfortunately, the communal aspect of salvation is not always appreciated. The church is not always thought to be essential to God's saving activity. Some people have been enthusiastic in praising Christianity and vehement in denouncing the church. It is not uncommon to hear such statements as "I love Jesus but I don't care for the church" or "I can be a better Christian without the church." Some have even espoused a "churchless Christianity."

What is the relation of the church to God's work of salvation? Is it central to His purpose, or is it an optional extra? The answer to these questions is found in the church's nature and mission.

The Church as Mission

The church is firmly rooted in the soil of Jesus' ministry. His intention was to create a community of people faithful to Him. His words, "I will build my church" (Matt. 16:18), express that purpose. Thus, Jesus' summons to all who heard him was "Follow me." The Gospels abound in references to this invitation (Mark 1:17; 2:14; 8:34; 10:21; Luke 9:59; John 1:43; compare 10:27; 12:26; 21:22).

From among those who followed Him, Jesus chose twelve men for a unique role. In Mark's Gospel we read, "He appointed twelve— designating them apostles—that they might be with him and that he might send them out to preach and to have authority to drive out demons" (3:14-15; compare Matt. 10:1-2; Luke 6:12-14). The number twelve corresponds to the number of the tribes of Israel. This was not an accident. These twelve apostles were the nucleus of a renewed Israel, the community in which the promise of the new covenant would be realized (compare Mark 14:24; Heb. 8:6-13). Jesus spent much of His time preparing the apostles for the ministry for which they were chosen.

On the Day of Pentecost, the risen Christ poured out the Spirit on His followers (Acts 1:4; 2:1-12). This event has sometimes been referred to as "the birthday of the church." Such a description does not deny the antecedents of the church in the Old Testament and the ministry of Jesus. It acknowledges that on this occasion the Spirit began to form the followers of Jesus into a dynamic body for bearing witness to Christ. It also recognizes that the church is supremely the community of the risen Christ. The church in the full New Testament sense is

grounded in the life, death, and resurrection of Christ. It also presupposes the powerful presence of the Holy Spirit.

The time between Pentecost and the consummation is time for the
mission of the church. That mission is to bear witness in word and
deed to God's saving work in Christ. Just before His ascension, Jesus
declared to His disciples, "But you will receive power when the Holy
Spirit comes on you; and you will be my witnesses in Jerusalem, and
in all Judea and Samaria, and to the ends of the earth" (Acts 1:8). The
Great Commission entrusted to the church is, "Therefore go and
make disciples of all nations, baptizing them in the name of the Father
and of the Son and of the Holy Spirit, and teaching them to obey
everything I have commanded you" (Matt. 28:19-20). Years after the
events recorded in Matthew 28 and Acts 1—2, Peter wrote to the
church scattered throughout the ancient world. He reminded them of
their identity and mission in these words: "But you are a chosen people, a royal priesthood, a holy nation, a people belonging to God, that
you may declare the praises of him who called you out of darkness
into his wonderful light" (1 Pet. 2:9; compare Ex. 19:5-6).

The mission of the church is essential to its nature. Mission is not
simply one option among others. Church without mission is a contradiction in terms. Thus, it is appropriate to say that the church *is* mission. This is what C. Norman Kraus means when he calls the church
"a movement rather than a religious society." He explains:

> The word movement suggests dynamic and action. A movement forms
> as a consequence of powerful convictions or events which call for
> action and change in response. Mission rather than organizational
> structure gives cohesiveness and form to a movement. Organization is
> secondary and is determined by the nature of the mission which actu-
> ally constitutes the movement.[12]

Insights from Images

The New Testament uses a number of images to portray the nature
of the church. There are approximately one hundred of these images.[13] In all of them, the church is related to the Triune God. It is
sufficient here to look at three of the most familiar descriptions.

The temple of God.—Paul used this image in two ways. (1) It desig-

nates the individual Christian whose body is a temple of the Holy
Spirit (1 Cor. 6:19). (2) Corporately it refers to believers who together form the church. "For we are the temple of the living God. As
God has said, 'I will live with them and walk among them, and I
will be their God'" (2 Cor. 6:16; compare 1 Cor. 3:16-17; Eph. 2:
19-22). The point is that God's presence is not in a temple made
with hands but in the midst of His people. This does not imply that
God's presence is confined to the church (compare 1 Kings 8:27; Jer.
23:23-24; Acts 17:24). But the church is the context in which His
presence is most clearly manifested and His saving purpose realized.

Peter also used temple imagery. "As you come to him, the living
Stone—rejected by men but chosen by God and precious to him—you
also, like living stones, are being built into a spiritual house to be a
holy priesthood, offering spiritual sacrifices acceptable to God
through Jesus Christ" (1 Pet. 2:4-5). Jesus is "the living Stone." He
was rejected and crucified. By virtue of His resurrection, He is alive
forever. Because of our relationship with the living Christ we, too,
become living stones. In union with Him, we are framed into a "spiritual house," a new temple as a dwelling place for God.

In this new temple, we are "a holy priesthood" for the purpose of
serving God. This is an important passage for the doctrine of the
priesthood of all believers. Under the old covenant only a selected
number from a single tribe served as priests. What was unheard of in
Judaism is basic to Christian faith. All converts enter the priesthood!
As Christians we are priests for ourselves and for others before God
(compare Rev. 1:5-6).

The activity of the new priesthood is to offer "spiritual sacrifices."
The old Temple was the place for offering animal sacrifices. All that
to which those sacrifices pointed has become a reality in the sacrifice
of Christ. Sacrifices offered in the new temple are a life of obedience (Rom. 12:1), thanksgiving and praise (Heb. 13:15), and service
(v. 16).

The body of Christ.—In this image, the church is compared to a
human body. Paul informed the Christians in Corinth, "Now you are
the body of Christ, and each one of you is part of it" (1 Cor. 12:27).
The same idea is conveyed to the Roman church. "Just as each of us

has one body with many members, and these members do not all have the same function, so in Christ we who are many form one body, and each member belongs to all the others" (Rom. 12:4-5). This imagery suggests the oneness of Christ with His people, the common life we share in Him and the interdependence of the members of the body.

In 1 Corinthians 12:14-26, Paul underlined the unity and diversity within the body. From this passage several truths emerge.

(1) We differ from one another. Each of us is unique, and each has a distinctive contribution to make to the body. Differences are not a weakness of the body; they are a potential strength. True unity is possible only as a result of diversity. Individuality is enhanced by finding our proper function in relation to other members of the body. It is individualism, not individuality, that is discouraged by the image of the body.

(2) We need one another. We reach our full potential as Christians only in community with other Christians. We should remember that the image of God has both vertical and horizontal dimensions. We were created for fellowship with God and other human beings. The restoration of the image in God's saving work involves both of these dimensions. Also, together we can accomplish more for Christ than any one of us can accomplish alone.

(3) We should care for one another. When one member hurts the whole body experiences pain. When one member rejoices all the members share the gladness. We are responsible for each other. In this mutual support and sharing the body grows in strength.

The image of the body does not imply that Christ *is* the church. In the unity there is also a distinction. The transcendence of Christ is preserved. Thus, Paul extended the image to include an emphasis on Christ as the Head of the church. "Christ is the head of the church, his body, of which He is the Savior" (Eph. 5:23; compare Col. 1:18).

The fellowship of the Spirit.—The benediction in 2 Corinthians 13:14 places fellowship alongside grace and love. "May the grace of the Lord Jesus Christ, and the love of God, and the fellowship of the Holy Spirit be with you all." The word *fellowship* means "sharing" "participation" or "holding in common." In the New Testament, its meaning is deeper than mere agreement or "a congenial fellowship of 'buddies.' "[14] It refers to our mutual sharing in the new life in Christ. As Christians, we share a common salvation, a common purpose, and a common hope.

The fellowship of the Spirit is a summary of the Spirit's varied activities in relation to the Christian life. The Spirit enables us to become Christians (1 Cor. 12:3). Through the Spirit, we become part of the body of Christ (v. 13). The Spirit is the basis of Christian assurance (Rom. 8:15-16) and the guarantee of our future inheritance (Eph. 1:13-14). Furthermore, the Spirit gives gifts for ministry (1 Cor. 12:11), empowers for service (Acts 1:8), and creates unity among believers (Eph. 4:3).

This Spirit-created fellowship is a divine gift rather than a human achievement. It involves two dimensions. Vertically, it involves fellowship with God. Paul reminded the Corinthians that God called them "into fellowship with his Son Jesus Christ our Lord" (1 Cor. 1:9). Similarly, John declared, "And our fellowship is with the Father and with his Son, Jesus Christ" (1 John 1:3). Horizontally, it involves fellowship with one another. The first converts to the Christian faith "devoted themselves to the apostles' teaching and to the fellowship, to the breaking of bread and to prayer" (Acts 2:42). When Peter, James, and John received Paul in Jerusalem, they extended the right hand of Christian fellowship (Gal. 2:9). John wrote, "We proclaim to you what we have seen and heard, so that you may have fellowship with us" (1 John 1:3). These two dimensions are interrelated. On the one hand, there can be no fellowship among believers apart from the fellowship of individuals with Christ. On the other hand, fellowship with Christ leads to fellowship among believers.

Given the nature and mission of the church, we can affirm two conclusions. (1) The church is not optional for the individual Christian. It is an essential part of God's saving activity. (2) The New Testament does not encourage free-lance Christianity. Salvation by its very nature is corporate as well as individual. Thus, Christ gave Himself "to purify for himself *a people that are his very own*" (Titus 2:14, author's italics).

Notes

1. Jack P. Scholfield, "Saved, Saved," 1975, no. 160.
2. For further reading see Gordon Clinard, *The Message We Proclaim* (Nashville: Convention Press, 1966), pp. 70-76; and W. T. Conner, *The Gospel of Redemption* (Nashville Broadman Press, 1945), pp. 139-145.
3. See the testimonies in Hugh T. Kerr and John M. Mulder, eds., *Conversions: The Christian Experience* (Grand Rapids: Wm. B. Eerdmans Publishing Co.), 1983.
4. Robert McAfee Brown, *The Spirit of Protestantism* (New York: Oxford University Press, 1965), p. 55.
5. Samuel Davies as quoted by J. I. Packer, *Knowing God* (Downer's Grove, Ill.: Inter-Varsity Press, 1973), pp. 121-122.
6. Martin Luther quoted by Brown, p. 61.
7. Good discussions of Paul and James on faith and works are found in the following sources: C. Leslie Mitton, *The Epistle of James* (Grand Rapids: Wm. B. Eerdmans Publishing Co., 1966), pp. 98-117; Peter H. Davids, *James*, "A Good News Commentary," W. Ward Gasque, ed. (San Francisco: Harper & Row Publishers, 1983), pp. 37-44.
8. Conner, p. 187.
9. For a good discussion of this theme, see Lewis B. Smedes, *Union With Christ*, 2nd ed., rev. (Grand Rapids: Wm. B. Eerdmans Publishing Co.), 1983.
10. Adolf Deissmann quoted by Ralph P. Martin, *Reconciliation; A Study of Paul's Theology,* "New Foundations Theological Library" (Atlanta: John Knox Press, 1980), p. 43.
11. George Eldon Ladd, *A Theology of the New Testament* (Grand Rapids: Wm. B. Eerdmans Publishing Co., 1974), pp. 482-483.
12. C. Norman Kraus, *The Community of the Spirit* (Grand Rapids: Wm. B. Eerdmans Publishing Co., 1974), pp. 38-39.
13. For a good treatment of this subject see Paul S. Minear, *Images of the Church in the New Testament* (Philadelphia: The Westminster Press), 1960.
14. Frank Stagg, *New Testament Theology* (Nashville: Broadman Press, 1962), p. 199.

Bibliography

Bloesch, Donald G. *The Christian Life and Salvation*. Grand Rapids: Wm. B. Eerdmans Publishing Co., 1967.

Clements, Keith. *Faith*. London: SCM Press, Ltd., 1981.

Crabtree, Arthur B. *The Restored Relationship*. Valley Forge: The Judson Press, 1963.

Ditmansen, Harold H. *Grace in Experience and Theology*. Minneapolis: Augsburg Publishing House, 1977.

Green, E. M. B. *The Meaning of Salvation*. Philadelphia: The Westminster Press, 1965.

Hordern, William, *Living by Grace*. Philadelphia: The Westminster Press, 1975.

Hunt, W. Boyd, "Toward a Doctrine of the Christian Life: An Evangelical Perspective," *Southwestern Journal of Theology* 20. Spring, 1978. :17-31.

Mackintosh. H. R. *The Christian Experience of Forgiveness*. London: Nisbet & Co., Ltd., 1941.

McDonald, H. D. *Salvation*. Westchester, Ill: Crossway Books, 1982.

Smyth, C. Ryder. *The Bible Doctrine of Salvation*. London: The Epworth Press, 1941.

7
The Consummation of Salvation

What is the world coming to? What can we expect in the future? What will happen to the human race? What will happen to me? The area of Christian doctrine which usually deals with these questions is eschatology. The word *eschatology* means the doctrine of last things. Insofar as the last things are future, eschatology is concerned with the future. This understanding of eschatology is true as far as it goes. We must remember, however, that the future cannot be separated from the past and present. The consummation of God's saving work is the fulfillment of all He has done in the past and is doing in the present.

Understood in this way, eschatology permeates every aspect of Christian faith. The Bible is an eschatological book. It is concerned with the fulfillment of God's work in the world. As we have seen, the Old Testament is a book of promise. It closes on a note of hope. It points to the action of God in Christ which is recorded in the New Testament. In one sense, the New Testament is a book of fulfillment. But the New Testament is also a book of promise. It, too, ends on a note of hope—the hope that its inspired vision of the future will be realized once and for all.

It is important to remember, however, that the Bible does not provide us with a detailed blueprint of future events. In His wisdom, God has revealed enough to sustain our hope and give us courage for the present. It is to our advantage that there are some things God has kept to Himself. As humans, we could not bear the burden of knowing all things in advance. Only a God who is all-powerful and all-wise can handle such knowledge responsibly.

Jesus encouraged His followers to live in hope, but He discouraged speculation. On one occasion He admitted, "No one knows about that day or hour, not even the angels in heaven, nor the Son, but only the Father" (Mark 13:32). Just before Jesus' ascension, a disciple asked Him about the future. Jesus responded, "It is not for you to know the times or dates the Father has set by his own authority" (Acts 1:7). The *fact* of the consummation is more important than the *time*.

Of course, God has not left us to grope in the dark. He has revealed what we need to know—no more or no less. Space prohibits a full discussion of eschatology.[1] Here we must be content to look at four themes which shape Christian hope.

The Second Coming of Christ

The second coming of Christ is not simply one theme among many which relates to the future. It is the very heart of the future. Paul referred to the expectation of the Lord's return as "the blessed hope" (Titus 2:13). Richard Longenecker reminds us that

> the Christian focuses upon the fully sufficient redemptive work of Christ in the past, the reign of Christ by His Spirit in the present, and the return of Christ to consummate God's redemptive purposes in the future. It is, therefore, the return of Christ that should be preeminent in the Christian's expectation and in his proclamation regarding the future.[2]

To speak of the second coming in the future does not mean that Christ is absent in the present. Before the ascension He promised the disciples, "Surely I will be with you always, to the very end of the age" (Matt. 28:20). Christ is present now in and through the Spirit. The Spirit is not a substitute for an absentee Lord but a confirmation of His presence in a new way. Though Christ is present, yet He is to come. The future coming is His visible, personal, and triumphant manifestation at the end of the age to consummate God's work of salvation.

The Promise of His Coming

The New Testament is saturated with references to the return of Christ. A brief survey of representative passages will help to put this promise in focus.

Several references occur in the teaching of Jesus. For example, to a crowd near Caesarea Philippi, He declared, "If anyone is ashamed of me and my words in this adulterous and sinful generation, the Son of Man will be ashamed of him when he comes in his Father's glory, with the holy angels" (Mark 8:38). To a group of His disciples, He explained, "At that time the sign of the Son of Man will appear in the sky, and all the nations of the earth will mourn. They will see the Son of Man coming on the clouds of the sky, with power and great glory" (Matt. 24:30; compare Mark 13:26; Luke 21:27). To the questioning of the high priest, He responded, "In the future you will see the Son of Man sitting at the right hand of the Mighty One and coming on the clouds of heaven" (Matt. 26:64; compare Mark 14:62). To His disciples in an upper room, Jesus offered these words of encouragement and promise:

> Do not let your hearts be troubled. Trust in God; trust also in me. In my Father's house are many rooms; if it were not so, I would have told you. I am going there to prepare a place for you. And if I go and prepare a place for you, I will come back and take you to be with me that you may also be where I am going (John 14:1-4).

Some interpreters believe that this passage refers to Christ's coming to His disciples in the Spirit. Others believe that it means His coming for them at the moment of death. It is true that the idea of "coming" may have various shades of meaning in John's Gospel. There is no reason, however, to rule out the second coming as the primary reference here. Jesus' final coming fulfills and completes the meaning of His other comings.[3]

A similar emphasis is found in Acts. When Jesus ascended to the Father, angelic messengers announced that "this same Jesus, who had been taken from you into heaven, will come back in the same way you have seen him go into heaven" (Acts1:11). There are allusions to the second coming in Peter's sermon at the Temple gate (3:19-21), in his witness to Cornelius (10:42), and in Paul's address to the Athenians (17:31).

The promise of Christ's return is reinforced in the letters of Paul. In Paul's earliest correspondence, 1 Thessalonians, there are several direct references. "For what is our hope, our joy, or the crown in which we will glory in the presence of our Lord Jesus when he comes?" (2:19). Paul prayed that God would strengthen their hearts so that they would be "blameless and holy in the presence of our God and Father when our Lord Jesus comes with all his holy ones" (3:13). Some members of the church were distressed about friends and loved ones who died before the consummation. Would they participate in Christ's final victory? Paul assured them that those who died would not be at a disadvantage.

> Brothers, we do not want you to be ignorant about those who fall asleep, or to grieve like the rest of men, who have no hope. We believe that Jesus died and rose again and so we believe that God will bring with Jesus those who have fallen asleep in him. According to the Lord's own word, we tell you that we who are still alive, who are left till the coming of the Lord, will certainly not precede those who have fallen asleep. For the Lord himself will come down from heaven, with a loud command, with the voice of the archangel and with the trumpet call of God, and the dead in Christ will rise first. After that, we who are still alive and are left will be caught up with them in the clouds to meet the Lord in the air. And so we will be with the Lord forever. Therefore encourage each other with these words (4:13-18).

The letter concludes with a reference to the promise and to God's faithfulness. "May your whole spirit, soul and body be kept blameless at the coming of our Lord Jesus Christ. The one who calls you is faithful and he will do it" (5:23-24).

References to Christ's return are not confined to Paul's earliest writing. He reminded the Philippians that "our citizenship is in heaven. And we eagerly await a Savior from there, the Lord Jesus Christ" (Phil. 3:20). Timothy was encouraged "to keep this commandment without spot or blame until the appearing of our Lord Jesus Christ" (1 Tim. 6:14). Furthermore, Timothy was challenged "In the presence of God and of Christ Jesus, who will judge the living and the dead, and in view of his appearing and his kingdom . . . Preach the Word" (2 Tim. 4:1-2). Titus was encouraged to practice and teach godly living "while we wait for the blessed hope—the glorious appearing of our great God and Savior, Jesus Christ" (Titus 2:13).

This same hope characterizes the Letter to the Hebrews. "So Christ was sacrificed once to take away the sins of many people; and he will appear a second time, not to bear sin, but to bring salvation to those who are waiting for him" (Heb. 9:28). Christ came the first time as the high priest to offer Himself as the sacrifice for sin. His second coming will be for a different purpose. Sin needs no further atonement. The return of Christ will be the final proof that His once-for-all sacrifice on the cross is eternally sufficient. At His return, He will bring to a conclusion the salvation we experience in the present.

Peter spoke of the future coming of Christ as an encouragement to steadfastness in trial and an incentive to selfless service (1 Pet. 1:7; 5:4). This hope is rooted in the person and work of Christ; it is not a fantasy created by Jesus' followers (2 Pet. 1:16-21). The Lord does not act according to human timetables. "With the Lord a day is like a thousand years, and a thousand years are like a day" (2 Pet. 3:8). If He does not come when we think He should, it is not because He has cancelled the appointment. Rather, it is because God is patient, "not wanting anyone to perish, but everyone to come to repentance" (v. 9). Christ's coming is certain because He is faithful in keeping His promises.

The Book of Revelation begins and ends with references to Christ's return. In the prologue we read, "Look, he is coming with the clouds, and every eye will see him, even those who pierced him; and all the people of the earth will mourn because of him" (1:7). At the close of the book we read, "He who testifies to these things says, 'Yes, I am coming soon.' Amen. Come, Lord Jesus" (22:20). Salvation history remains incomplete until Christ returns.

The Purpose of His Coming

Christ is coming to complete what He began. This does not mean that His first coming was inadequate and that He must return to make up for deficiencies. Rather, the two comings are distinguishable parts of one great work of salvation. Because of the nature and purpose of the first coming, the second was implicit in it from the beginning.

He is coming to complete His work in us.—In the last chapter we saw that salvation is in three tenses—past, present, and future. We have been saved (conversion). We are being saved (growth). We shall be saved (maturity). In light of the dynamic nature of salvation, any claim to present perfection is premature. We are assured that "he who began a good work in you will carry it on to completion until the day of Christ Jesus" (Phil. 1:6). The final outcome of salvation will be revealed when Christ returns (Col. 1:28; 1 Pet. 1:5; 1 John 3:2).

What is true of our individual lives is also true of our corporate life in church. Christ's purpose is "to present her to himself as a radiant church, without stain or wrinkle or any other blemish, but holy and blameless" (Eph. 5:27; compare Rev. 19:7-8). It is evident that the church as we experience it now falls short of this ideal. Christ's goal for the church, however, should be a source of continual encouragement.

He is coming to complete His victory over evil.—The second coming will mark the final conquest over all that is evil. Paul explained that the end will come when Christ "hands over the kingdom to God the Father after he has destroyed all dominion, authority and power. For he must reign until he has put all his enemies under his feet. The last enemy to be destroyed is death" (1 Cor. 15:24-26). Christ's "enemies" are all the forces which seek to hinder His saving work. "Destroy" here means "to bring to nothing." The thought is that Christ's victory over these forces is absolute and complete. This is reinforced by the scene in Revelation 20:7-15 which envisions the final defeat of the devil, death, and all who oppose God's purpose.

Many New Testaments passages assert that the essential victory over evil was won at Christ's first coming. (Matt. 28:18; John 12:31; Col. 2:14-15; 1 John 3:8). At this point it is helpful to remember the illustration of D day and V-day. The decisive battle has been fought. At His second coming Christ will bring to its fullness the victory which was won in His life, death, and resurrection.

It would be difficult to overestimate the significance of this hope. Just as everything depended on His first coming, everything also depends on His return. Apart from the hope of a final victory the struggle with sin is inconclusive, death remains an undefeated foe, and the

problem of suffering is insoluble. What Paul said about Christ's resurrection, we may also say about His second coming. "If only for this
life we have hope in Christ, we are to be pitied more than all men"
(1 Cor. 15:19).

The Resurrection of the Dead

A major result of Christ's second coming is the resurrection of the
dead. This is our hope in the face of death, the last enemy to be
destroyed (1 Cor. 15:26). Resurrection is the promise that though
physical death is inevitable, it cannot diminish the eternal life we have
in Christ.

The Hope of Resurrection

Resurrection hope began to emerge in the Old Testament. For example, "He will swallow up death forever. The Sovereign Lord will
wipe away the tears from all faces" (Isa. 25:8). "But your dead will
live; their bodies will rise. You who dwell in the dust, wake up and
shout for joy" (26:19). "Multitudes who sleep in the dust of the earth
will awake: some to everlasting life, others to shame and everlasting
contempt" (Dan. 12:2). Though resurrection is not explicit, there are
psalms which express hope for deliverance from Sheol, the place of
the dead (Ps. 16:9-11; 49:5; 73:24). Such expressions, whether resurrection is implicit or explicit, are rooted in the belief that God is the
living God who will not abandon His people to death. Nevertheless, it
remained for the New Testament to bring these pointers into clearer
focus.

That clearer focus is evident in John's Gospel. Jesus warned the
Jews of a time "when all who are in their graves will hear his voice
and come out—those who have done good will rise to live, and those
who have done evil will rise to be condemned" (5:28-29). Similarly,
in 6:39-40, 44, and 54, He spoke of a resurrection "at the last day."
In response to Martha's reference to the future resurrection, Jesus
made a remarkable claim. "I am the resurrection and the life. He
who believes me will live, even though he dies; and whoever lives and
believes in me will never die" (11:25). Eternal life, the life of the age
to come, cannot be touched by death.

In Paul's Epistles, the resurrection is presented at greatest length (compare the section on "The Basis of Resurrection Hope" in ch. 5). His most detailed discussion is in 1 Corinthians 15. For Paul, the resurrection of Christ was not an isolated event. As the resurrected One, Christ is the firstfruits of a greater harvest to come. Our future is interwined with His. Paul explained that

> Christ has indeed been raised from the dead, the firstfruits of those who have fallen asleep. For since death came through a man, the resurrection of the dead comes also through a man. For as in Adam all die, so in Christ all will be made alive. But each in his own turn: Christ, the firstfruits; then, when he comes, those who belong to him (vv. 20-23).

The Nature of the Resurrection Body

Discussion of the resurrection raises two related questions. "How are the dead raised? With what kind of body will they come?" (1 Cor. 15:35). The question of *how* is answered by affirming the wisdom and power of God. Paul illustrated his answer from three areas of the created order. The illustrations include plant life (vv. 37-38), the animal world (v. 39) and the heavenly bodies (vv. 40-41). The point of these illustrations is that in His wisdom and power God has given to each created thing a body appropriate to its nature and function. If God can fashion bodies perfectly adapted to this age, He can also provide bodies perfectly fitted for the age to come.

The question of *what kind* is approached by a series of contrasts between our present bodies and the body we will have in the resurrection.

(1) There is a contrast between the perishable and the imperishable (v. 42). Our present bodies are subject to disease and decay. They are mortal and will eventually turn to dust. Our resurrection bodies will be free from these limitations.

(2) There is a contrast between dishonor and glory (v. 43). This does not mean that it is dishonorable to have a body. But our present bodies show the effects of our sin. Our resurrection bodies will be unmarred by sin.

(3) There is a contrast between weakness and power (v. 43). The

most glaring weakness of our present bodies is their inability to resist death. Our resurrection bodies will be free from all handicaps and will not be subject to death.

(4) There is a contrast between the natural body and the spiritual body (v. 44). Ray Summers points out that this verse is the heart of everything that Paul said about the nature of the resurrection body. Summers writes, "Paul's insistence was that the eternal state will be a bodily state, even as the temporal state has been a bodily state. He did not say that there is planted a *body* and raised a *spirit*. He said there is planted a *natural body* and raised a *spiritual body*" (italics his).[4]

Where did Paul get his model for the resurrection body? The most likely suggestion is found in Philippians 3:20-21. "But our citizenship is in heaven. And we eagerly await a Savior from there, the Lord Jesus Christ, who by the power that enables him to bring everything under his control, will transform our lowly bodies so that *they will be like his glorious body*" (author's italics).

What is the relationship between our present selves and our future, resurrected selves? (1) There is *continuity*. Our identities are not destroyed. We will be the same persons. This continuity enables us to believe that we will recognize one another in the eternal state. (2) There is also *discontinuity*. We will be the same persons with a difference. (3) The difference is due to *transformation*. God will transform us so that we can become what we were intended to be and realize our true potential as children of God.

In dramatic language Paul envisioned the moment of transformation:

Listen, I tell you a mystery: We will not all sleep, but we will all be changed—in a flash, in the twinkling of an eye, at the last trumpet. For the trumpet will sound, the dead will be raised imperishable, and we will be changed. For the perishable must clothe itself with the imperishable, and the mortal with immortality. When the perishable has been clothed with the imperishable, and the mortal with immortality, then the saying that is written will come true: "Death has been swallowed up in victory." "Where, O death is your victory? Where, O death, is your sting?" The sting of death is sin, and the power of sin is the law. But thanks be to God! He gives us the victory through our Lord Jesus Christ (1 Cor. 15:51-56).

The Last Judgment

The Reality of Judgment

Resurrection is a prelude to the last judgment. This note of a final accounting is sounded repeatedly in the New Testament (Matt. 25:32; Acts 10:42; 17:31; Heb. 10:30; Jas. 5:9; Rev. 20:12). Simply stated, the last judgment means that "We must all appear before the judgment seat of Christ, that each one may receive what is due him for the things done while in the body, whether good or bad" (2 Cor. 5:10).

Some New Testament passages say that God the Father will judge (1 Peter 1:7; Rom. 14:10; Matt. 18:35; 1 Thess. 1:5). Other emphasize that Christ will judge (John 5:22; 2 Tim. 4:8; Acts 10:42; 2 Cor. 5:10). There is no contradiction among these declarations. The New Testament stresses the unity of Father and Son in creation (John 1:4), salvation (2 Cor. 5:19) and judgment. Paul informed the Athenians that God "has set a day when he will judge the world with justice by the man he has appointed" (Acts 17:31). The same thought is expressed in Romans 2:16. "This will take place on the day when God will judge men's secrets through Jesus Christ."

The last judgment is the consummation of the judgment that is already in progress. Judgment as present and future is emphatic in John's Gospel. "And this is the judgment, that the light has come into the world, and men loved darkness rather than light because their deeds were evil" (John 3:19, RSV).

"Now is the time for judgment on the world; now the prince of this world will be driven out" (John 12:31). The future is emphasized in verse 48. "There is a judge for the one who rejects me and does not accept my words; that very word which I spoke will condemn him at the last day."

Believers and the Judgment

The ultimate basis for judgment is one's relationship to Christ. As those who are trusting in Christ for salvation, we can approach the final day with assurance. Our assurance, however, is not in ourselves. It is in the Judge Himself. God, the Judge, is the One who "so loved the world that he gave his one and only Son" (John 3:16). Christ, the

Judge, is the One who loved us and gave Himself for us (Gal. 2:20). The Judge is not neutral. He is for us, not against us.

In Christ we have already received the verdict of acquittal (Rom. 8:1). Thus, we have confidence that this verdict will be confirmed at the final day. In fact, we are encouraged to have this confidence by these words:

> If God is for us, who can be against us? He who did not spare his own Son, but gave him up for us all—how will he not also, along with him, graciously give us all things? Who will bring any charge against those whom God has chosen? It is God who justifies. Who is he that condemns? Christ Jesus, who died—more than that, who was raised to life—is at the right hand of God and is also interceding for us. Who shall separate us from the love of Christ? Shall trouble or hardship or persecution or famine or nakedness or danger or sword? As it is written:
>
>> "For your sake we face death all day long;
>> we are considered as sheep to be slaughtered."
>
> No, in all these things we are more than conquerors through him who loved us. For I am convinced that neither death nor life, neither angels nor demons, neither the present nor the future, nor any powers, neither height nor depth, nor anything else in all creation, will be able to separate us from the love of God that is in Christ Jesus our Lord (Rom. 8:31-39).

Unbelievers and the Judgment

The last judgment marks the final separation between believers and unbelievers. Unbelievers "will go away to eternal punishment, but the righteous to eternal life" (Matt. 25:46). It is tragic to think of anyone being finally excluded from the kingdom of God. Nevertheless, it is a part of New Testament teaching (Matt. 13:30, 39-43; 25:31-46; Rev. 20:11-25).

The biblical word which describes this exclusion is *hell*. The reality of hell is described in dreadful terms throughout the New Testament. It is "where 'their worm does not die, and the fire is not quenched'" (Mark 9:48; compare Isa. 66:24). It is "the darkness, where there will be weeping and gnashing of teeth" (Matt. 8:12), "where fire never goes out" (Mark 9:44), the "fiery furnace" (Matt. 13:42), and "eternal fire" (Matt. 18:18). Hell is the "blackest darkness," "perishing" (2 Thess. 2:10), the second death which is the lake of fire (Rev. 20:14; 21:8). Caution should be used in interpreting these symbols. But to say it is symbolic does not mean that it isn't real. As one writer states, "If hell is not fire, it is something infinitely worse. No wonder Jesus warned against it so often and so emphatically."[5]

The reality of hell reminds us that we are responsible for the way we use our freedom. God did not create robots to be manipulated. He created persons capable of freely responding to Him. Freedom is His gift to us. God desires our willing response. He woos us, but He does not force us. "Becoming a child of God is an opportunity offered, never a relationship imposed."[6] The tragedy of hell is the abuse of freedom to reject the God who gave the freedom. This results in separation from redemptive fellowship with God. The horror of hell is realized when the separation becomes final.

New Heavens and New Earth

The Bible begins, "In the beginning God created the heavens and the earth" (Gen. 1:1). It ends with the expectation of new heavens and a new earth. God's work is not only to save individuals but also to redeem the whole creation from the effects of sin. His saving work will not be complete until the new earth has been ushered in. Thus, Paul wrote,

> The creation waits in eager expectation for the sons of God to be revealed. For the creation was subjected to frustration, not by its own choice, but by the will of the one who subjected it, in hope that the creation itself will be liberated from its bondage to decay and brought into the glorious freedom of the children of God (Rom. 8:19-21).

Similarly, Peter declared, "But in keeping with his promise we are looking forward to a new heaven and a new earth, the home of righteousness" (2 Pet. 3:13).

God creates the new earth as a suitable dwelling place for His redeemed people. The caricature of heaven as a place where ghostlike

forms sit on clouds, plucking harps, is just that—a caricature. Most
of the New Testament references to God's final victory focuses upon
the earth, "the earth transformed into that place of man's habitation
purposed by God from the first."[7]

> Then I saw a new heaven and a new earth, for the first heaven and the
> first earth had passed away, and there was no longer any sea. I saw the
> Holy City, the new Jerusalem, coming down out of heaven from God,
> prepared as a bride beautifully dressed for her husband. And I heard a
> loud voice from the throne saying, "Now the dwelling of God is with
> men, and he will live with them. They will be his people, and God
> himself will be with them and be their God. He will wipe every tear
> from their eyes. There will be no more death or mourning or crying or
> pain, for the old order of things has passed away" (Rev. 21:1-4).

What is the relationship of the new earth to the old one? Is everything in the old order destroyed? Is nothing carried over into the new
order? The New Testament does not give explicit answers to these
questions. On the basis of what we know of God's saving work, however, we may venture a suggestion. The relationship is one of continuity and discontinuity. Consider thoughtfully the following statement:

> We have already seen . . . how Paul speaks in 1 Corinthians 15 of
> the continuity of our personalities through death into resurrection.
> There is a parallel continuity of what we may loosely term "culture."
> Revelation 21:26 says, "The greatness and the wealth of the nations
> will be brought into the city. But nothing that is impure will enter the
> city." This suggests that, because God is a creative God who affirms
> the goodness of the world he has made, he will not simply write it off
> with all its wealth of art and beauty and human inventiveness. In God's
> economy nothing is wasted. All the creative work of men and women
> which reflects the abundant creativity of God will be carried over into
> the transformed world. We can only guess at how this may be. But it
> tells us something of how God values the creative work of men and
> women—much of it produced out of suffering and at great personal
> cost. And it is another sign that the world to come is not a colorless,
> shadowy existence, but a totally fulfilling world, worthy of its creator.[8]

In the meanwhile we live in gratitude and hope fixing "our eyes on
Jesus, the author and perfector of our faith" (Heb. 12:2).

Notes

1. For a detailed treatment of eschatology see the books listed in the bibliography for this chapter. A future volume in this series will treat the numerous topics which pertain to this subject.
2. Richard N. Longenecker, "The Return of Christ" in *Handbook of Biblical Prophecy,* ed. Carl E. Armerding and W. Ward Gasque (Grand Rapids: Baker Book House, 1977), pp. 149-150.
3. Ray Summers, *Behold the Lamb* (Nashville: Broadman Press, 1979), pp. 179, 187.
4. Ray Summers, *The Life Beyond,* pp. 68-69.
5. Herschel H. Hobbs, *Fundamentals of Our Faith* (Nashville: Broadman Press, 1960), p. 146.
6. Frank Stagg, *New Testament Theology,* p. 334.
7. Walter Harrelson, "God's Purpose for the Church," *Religion in Life* Spring, 1963, p. 84.
8. Stephen H. Travis, *I Believe in the Second Coming of Jesus,* p. 181.

Bibliography

Baker, Nelson B. *What is the World Coming To?* Philadelphia: The Westminster Press, 1965.

Beasley-Murray, G. R. *Jesus and the Future.* London: Macmillan and Co., 1954; reprint ed., 1956.

Bryson, Harold T. *The Reality of Hell and the Goodness of God.* Wheaton, Illinois: Tyndale House Publishers, Inc., 1984.

Ewert, David. *And Then Comes the End.* Scottdale, Pennsylvania: Herald Press, 1980.

Hoekema, Anthony A. *The Bible and the Future.* Grand Rapids: William B. Eerdmans Publishing Co., 1979.

Ladd, George Eldon. *The Last Things: An Eschatology for Laymen.* Grand Rapids: William B. Eerdmans Publishing Co., 1978.

Milne, Bruce. What the Bible Teaches About the End of the World. *The Layman's Series.* Ed. by G. W. Kirby. Wheaton, Illinois: Tyndale House Publishers, Inc., 1979.

Moody, Dale. *The Hope of Glory.* Grand Rapids: William B. Eerdmans Publishing Co., 1964.

Strawson, William. *Jesus and the Future Life.* Philadelphia: The Westminster Press, 1959.

Summers, Ray. *The Life Beyond*. Nashville: Broadman Press, 1959.
Travis, Stephen H. *I Believe in the Second Coming of Jesus*. Grand Rapids: William B. Eerdmans Publishing Co., 1982.

Scripture Index